The Military Orchid

Jocelyn Brooke

Illustrated by
Gavin Bone and Stephen Bone

LITTLE TOLLER BOOKS
an imprint of THE DOVECOTE PRESS

This paperback edition published in 2011 by
Little Toller Books
Stanbridge, Wimborne Minster, Dorset BH21 4JD
First published in 1948 by The Bodley Head

ISBN 978-1-908213-05-1

Typeset in Monotype Sabon by Little Toller Books
Printed in Spain by GraphyCems, Navarra

All papers used by Little Toller Books and the Dovecote Press
are natural, recyclable products made from
wood grown in sustainable, well-managed forests

A CIP catalogue record for this book is available
from the British Library

1 3 5 7 9 8 6 4 2

CONTENTS

FOREWORD

John Urmston

U NCLE BERNARD – as Jocelyn Brooke was known to me – had a mania for making home-made fireworks. When I was five years old he taught me how to screw up a few chemicals in a cigarette paper and hit it with a hammer. Bang! Once, when Uncle Bernard had gone out, I tried the same experiment on my own: I didn't have any cigarette papers and put the chemicals into a paper bag, adding a few extra ingredients for good measure. The result was an explosion which blew me on to my back and rattled the windows.

Not to be outdone by a child, Uncle Bernard attempted a bomb using rolled-up cardboard packed with chemicals and fitted with a fuse of saltpetre. He placed the device on the lawn as we hurried to the safety of the house. He lit it. There was a puff of smoke, then nothing. Under the baleful glances of my father, armed with coal tongs and wearing a copper scuttle on his head, Uncle Bernard then walked across the lawn like a crusader and picked up the smouldering beast, depositing it in water at the bottom of the garden where it expired with a gurgle.

To go on a country walk with Uncle Bernard was a joy (and somewhat safer). He knew the names of all the wild flowers, and often their medicinal qualities too. He also taught me to appreciate French music, particularly Ravel, Debussy and Poulenc, whose *Mouvements perpétuels* he played for me, rather badly, on the piano. When I was a teenager he decided to broaden my horizons by taking me to London for an Italian lunch at Bertorelli in Soho. We had risotto. He ordered a Chianti for himself and a Sauternes for me. After lunch we went to the Fitzroy pub nearby, where the clientele were mostly writers and artists, like the Queen of Bohemia herself, Nina Hamnett. Afterwards we went to watch *Les Enfants du Paradis* at the cinema, to continue my 'education', but the day must have already been a bit much for me: I fell asleep and woke as the closing credits began to roll.

John Urmston
Salisbury, 2011

Orchis
Mascula
Early Purple Orchid.

INTRODUCTION

Horatio Clare

I ASKED A FAMOUS AUTHOR what she desired, now that she had had a worldwide best-seller.

'Oh, I just want to write one good book,' she said. 'My ambition is to be a decent English novelist.'

A couple of years later she produced *On Beauty*, and few would deny her success – Zadie Smith is a decent English novelist, by any standard. I asked another superstar, the French novelist Anna Gavalda (even more successful there, and in many other countries, than Smith is here) what she aimed for.

'But it's obvious,' she said. 'We must inform ourselves, then we try to write a masterpiece. That is the job, no?'

By either of these measures, then, Jocelyn Brooke was a success. And yet: who remembers Brooke now? Who read him then? Brooke's springboard and central subject – his own life – does not automatically suggest an oeuvre made for immortality. He did not take to education, running away twice before he was withdrawn: 'My public school career lasted a fortnight, which may, for all I know, constitue a record.'

After a happier stint at Bedales he went to university where he self-published *Six Poems*. 'When I got to Oxford I was totally unable to construe a simple bit of Latin prose, and consequently distinguished myself by failing in the Law Prelim at the end of my first year.' Brooke is sent down. He writes but publishes nothing.

The war sees him working in a venereal disease unit of the Medical
Corps. Demobbed, he produces another volume of poetry and joins
his father's business, which allows him to try his hand at failing as
a wine merchant. Having more or less botched civilian life, he re-
enlists in the army – to general mystification.

> 'Say, are you the bloke that signed on again?'
> 'Yes, that's me.'
> 'Cor, stone a crow. What did you do it for – was the police after
> you?'
> 'No – at least I don't think they were.'
> 'Come on Andy, get weaving.'
> 'It's half twelve,' said Andy, who had lit a fag and picked up the
> *Mirror.*
> 'So it is and all – another morning gone,' said the corporal. 'Sixty-six
> and a half days more before my demob – and by Christ,' he added,
> with a grin at me, 'they won't get me back.'

And then, in 1948, The Bodley Head publishes Brooke's little
masterpiece, a queer species of autobiography called *The Military
Orchid*. The critics are delighted by it; a discerning section of the
public enjoy it; Brooke is able to buy himself out of the army; the
BBC give him a job as a talks producer – one might think his orchid
had flowered. But no: unhappy in London and the job, Brooke lasts
four months, resigns and moves to Ivy Cottage, Bishopsbourne,
where he lives with Ninnie, the strict Baptist nanny who raised him.
From now on, he writes. Criticism, reviews, a torrent of books pour
from his pen: non-fiction (botany); novels (many are variations of
autobiography, with twists); autobiography (two more volumes
complete *The Orchid Trilogy*: a mosaic of truth, fiction and
fictionalisation); surrealist pastiche (imagine his publisher's reaction
on being handed *The Crisis in Bulgaria, or, Ibsen to the Rescue!* in
1956) and at least one true novel, *The Image of a Drawn Sword*.

Anthony Powell – who reviewed the second volume of the *Orchid Trilogy* for *The Times Literary Supplement* – believed Jocelyn Brooke 'one of the notable writers to have surfaced after the war'. *The Image of a Drawn Sword*, Powell said, 'is not in its way, inferior to Kafka', and he noted that despite its haunting, dystopic qualities Brooke had read no Kafka when he wrote it. John Betjeman complimented Brooke on being 'as subtle as the devil'. Eizabeth Bowen said 'His writing is imaginatively unique . . . a great writer'. But if Brooke dies a *succès d'estime* he also leaves the stage without due recognition, unburdened by fortune or glory. Penguin republish *The Orchid Trilogy* in 1981, copies of which survive still in the shelves of the seriously bibliophilic, but that, until now, was that.

The forgotten, the overlooked, the bypassed writer is a favourite subject with writers; theirs is a melancholy fate which haunts many of us in our darker hours and awaits pretty well all in the end. We are drawn to such figures because they are mournfully comforting reflections of the cold vagaries of fortune, the hot, short tastes of fame and the idiosyncratic favours of culture. But the nearly-man or woman of letters is a hackneyed figure, not nearly as interesting as its coefficient – the writer who never achieves the magnified life of a Gavalda or a Smith, whose works never thunder into posthumous fashion, but who, nevertheless, refuses to die. It takes something special to be numbered among these particular creatures, to smoulder on despite a fuse which never quite flared. Your work will have to speak powerfully and memorably to the few who encounter it. At least one or two of your books, which will probably be strange fish, even by the standards of books, will have to be very good indeed. Welcome, then, to the quietly dazzling talent of Jocelyn Brooke.

I was more interested, at that time, in flowers than in people. Indeed, except in particular cases, I still am. Yet the social flora of the Sandgate

Undercliff, where we lived, was perhaps worthy of study. I devoted to it approximately the same amount of attention as I did to bird life – a subject which I found less interesting than flowers or butterflies, but not without a certain attraction.

It was seldom, in the social milieu frequented by my family, that I encountered anything so exotic and orchidaceous as Miss Trumpett.

Brooke is vastly easy to like and not simply because his prose is so elegant, and every paragraph has a flower, a twist or a sweet one-liner in its tail. He has beguiling passions for Proust, wine, Italy, words, Dover, soldiers, French, music, and first equal above all, orchids and fireworks. In *A Mine of Serpents*, his second volume of autobiography, which takes its name from a firework, he meets a stranger on a train:

> This shared mania, this *amour qui n'ose pas dire son nom*, was none other than a shared passion for . . . fireworks. We were, both of us, chronic pyrotechnomaniacs. We loved fireworks to the point of imbecility – fireworks of all kinds, from Brock's Benefit at the Crystal Palace to the humble half-crown's worth in the back garden. It is not a common vice among adut males; its Freudian interpretation may well be sinister . . .'

The playful innuendo is not, I think, Brooke sending lightly coded signals, so much as signalling as explicitly as he decently can, given the absurd laws and oppressions of his time: not far below the surface of the *Trilogy* is a story of Brooke's heart-life, all the more moving because it cannot be recounted aloud. His account of Miss Trumpett concludes with a delightfully subtle-unsubtle confession: 'Obscurely, perhaps, I felt that I wasn't cut out for such as Miss Trumpett; her world was too alien, too romantically remote.'

Brooke's dislikes are equally entertaining. He has such an apalled dread of bores that he becomes fascinated by one called Basil, whom Brooke adopts – meeting Basil, studying Basil, sponging off Basil and drinking a great deal with Basil in a committed attempt to

assess the limits of Basil's capacity to bore. This is a respectable sort
of activity for Futilitarians: Brooke is an adamant and 'impenitent'
Futilitarian. He explains that a Man of the Twenties (like T.S.
Eliot's Prufrock) lived in a kind of timeless St Martin's Summer,
in an epoch isolated by the First World War, the Boom and the
Slump, 'in which the past was forgotten, and the future, as far as
possible, ignored'. Brooke offers no definition of Futilitarianism,
presumably on the grounds that explaining to any who might
require explantion would be futile, but he says the Twenties failed
to prepare its adherents for 'the drab and earnest salvationism'
of the Thirties. The 'extraordinary decade', Brooke says, renders
many of its young men incurably nostalgic and imbues them with
only one ethical slogan – Intellectual Honesty. So Brooke is not
being misanthropic when he says he is more interested in flowers
than people; he is not even slighting people, really – it just happens
that he loves, adores and worships flowers. Not all flowers, though.
'Whole tracts of the subject leave me cold: certain families or genera
frankly bore me, and always will – the Chenopodiaceae, for example,
or those tedious *Hieracii*, or the chickweeds.'

Apart from his impeccable rythms, diction and timing, which
would make his work a joy to read aloud, another of the qualities
which make Jocelyn Brooke a superb and superbly pleasurable
writer is his frank dismissal of great swathes of creation and
existence, a discernment which allows him to better concentrate on
the bits that do appeal.

Against the hot blue sky, the terraced knoll loomed enormous, its
summit lost in a shimmering heat-haze. The grassy flanks seemed to
radiate a reflected heat, enfolding us in a weighted, thyme-scented
silence, enhanced rather than disturbed by the monotone of a thousand
insects. On the banks at the hill's foot, the cropped turf was gemmed
with the small downland flowers, many of which I had never seen

before: rockrose, milkwort, centaury. In that moment, I encountered a new Love – the chalkdown flora: a Love to which I have always remained faithful. Most botanists have their ecological preferences; and though I have had brief spells of infidelity with peat bogs, with sand dunes or even with wealden clay, the downs remain my Cynara, and I still return to them with some of the pristine delight of that first visit to The Hills.

Graham Greene may have been correct in his assertion that a writer requires a splinter of ice in his heart, but a good one also needs passionate fire, the passion of Brooke's capitalised Love.

A miniature chalkpit dazzled our eyes a little way up the hill. Running ahead, I paused near the edge of it: a plant had caught my eye, a flower with pink petals on which a bee seemed to be resting. Suddenly I realised that this was the goal of our pilgrimage; like Langhorne,

I sought the living bee to find
And found the picture of a bee.

Yes, there was no doubt of it: a single plant, standing stiff and aloof, bearing proudly aloft its extraordinary insect-flowers, like archaic jewels rifled from some tomb; I had found the bee orchid.

This is great writing and great nature writing because it flows from the thing itself – life lived; the intensity of conscious existence in the world. It is not a forced and adjectival attempt to inflate and stretch language until it obtains something of the width and colour of the world (which, forced, it never does). Rather, it is a simple product of a sensibility which is itself part linguistic, part scientific, part musical and part visual. It is this rare combination of sensitivity and facility which makes a great writer about nature, an H.E. Bates, or a BB; a Richard Jefferies, a Kathleen Jamie, Richard Mabey or Jim Perrin. Extraordinary writing about the world cannot be forced, but nor does it come hard to those who exist in the world in the way these writers do. Writing, for Brooke, is not an alternative or an addition to life but a completion of it. Reading him, like reading any of these writers at their best, is to share the experience of a completed life – not in a linear sense but in terms of depth and breadth. Look again at his 'weighted, thyme-scented silence'. It seems to expand from horizon to (unmentioned) horizon, filling the mind's eye with a scene, almost an epoch, which is not so much described as transmitted. When I teach nature writing I sometimes suggest, perhaps mischievously, that writing is actually walking, after which the creation of a book or piece is just a question of typing.

A reader on the cusp of discovering *The Military Orchid*, itself such a deceptively light creation, should not be burdened with a weighty introduction. There is much more one would wish to say of Jocelyn Brooke, but one imagines him (immaculately tailored) eyeing one speculatively, thinking, *oh dear me, another bore . . .* His book will sing to any who will open it: my own first experience was one of amazed and delighted recognition. How could I have so much in common with such a singular man? I am shamefully ignorant of flowers, but this book does not seem to be about them any more or less than it is about childhood, the army, about England, about Sicily, about tramping around Italy hopefully asking '*Avete del vino?*', about being not quite in and not quite out of the world, about loves which you can explain only implicitly, about the supreme comedy of other people – about nothing, in the end, but life.

Horatio Clare
Verona, 2011

Souldiers Satyrion bringeth forth many broad large and ribbed leaves, spread upon the ground like unto those of the great Plantaine: among the which riseth up a fat stalke full of sap or juice, clothed or wrapped in the like leaves even to the tuft of flowers, wherupon do grow little flowers resembling a little man, having a helmet upon his head, his hands and legs cut off; white upon the inside, spotted with many purple spots, and the back part of the flower of a deeper colour tending to rednes. The rootes be greater stones than any of the kinds of Satyrions.

GERARD, *Herball*, 1597

I have found it during the last four years very sparingly. It only appeared in a barren state in 1886.

G.C. DRUCE, *Flora of Oxfordshire*

Orchis militaris shows its close affinity with O. *purpurea*, perhaps, by sharing its sterility, though this appears to be less pronounced on the Continent . . .

EDWARD STEP, *Wayside and Woodland Blossoms*

Rare in Spring. Grows in chalky districts only and not always there.

J.S.E. MACKENZIE, *British Orchids*

Now nearly extinct.

M.J. GODFERY, *Monograph and Iconograph of Native British Orchidaceae*

AUTHOR'S NOTE

THIS BOOK is not, strictly, an autobiography, and the author has taken a novelist's liberties both with persons and institutions. I hope that 'St Ethelbert's' and schools of its kind have long ceased to exist; as for the dramatis personae, so far as they impinge upon reality at all, they are to be considered as caricatures rather than characters.

J.B.

PART ONE

A Box of Wormseed

Thou art a box of wormseed,
at best but a salvatory of green mummy.

DUCHESS OF MALFI

M R BUNDOCK'S FUNCTION, so far as my family was concerned, was to empty the earth-closet twice a week at the cottage where we used to spend the summer. This duty he performed unobtrusively and usually late at night: looming up suddenly in the summer dusk, earth-smelling and hairy like some menial satyr, a kind of Lob. (Perhaps the maids left a bowl of cream for him on the threshold.) He became of sudden interest to me one June evening by asserting, quite calmly, that he had found the lizard orchid.

Now the lizard orchid, at that period, had just made one of its rare appearances in the district: mysterious and portentous as the return of a comet, but, unlike a comet, unpredictable. A photograph of its extraordinary bearded spike had appeared in the *Folkestone Herald*; the finder was an elderly Folkestone photographer, who had subsequently exhibited the plant in his shop window, where I had been taken to see it. Very kindly, he had detached two florets from the spike and presented them to me. (I heard, many years afterwards, that he was suspected of importing plants from the Continent and naturalising them on the hills near Folkestone. The story recalls Gerard, who glibly asserted, in the 1597 edition of his *Herball*, that he had found the wild peony in Kent; a statement corrected in the 1633 edition by Johnson, who explains that Gerard 'himselfe planted the Peonie there, and afterwards seemed to find it there by accident.')

Mr Bundock seemed to think nothing of finding the lizard. One might have supposed it was an everyday occurrence with him. He promised to bring me specimens the next evening. I waited with immense excitement. He duly arrived, and presented me with several specimens of the 'lizard orchid'. Alas! it was not the lizard at all, but the green man orchid, *Aceras anthropophorum*: a rarity, certainly, but not to be compared with the almost mythical lizard. Besides, I had already found it myself.

My disappointment was immense, but mitigated by the other orchid which Mr Bundock had brought me. This was unfamiliar: a tall, handsome spike of purple-brown and pink-spotted flowers. Obviously, I thought, it came under the desirable category of Very Rare Orchids. But which was it?

I must have been about seven years old at this period; and besides being a keen (if somewhat erratic) botanist, I had already begun to specialise: I was bitten with the orchid-mania. Up till this time, the only 'flower book' I had possessed was Edward Step's *Wayside and Woodland Blossoms*: adequate for the amateur, but not of much service to the specialist. On my seventh birthday, however, I had acquired a book on the orchids themselves: *British Orchids, How to Tell One from Another*, by a certain Colonel Mackenzie. I still possess the book: produced in a rather sub-arty style, it bears no publication date, and must have been long out of print. It is illustrated with a dozen watercolours, mostly of the commoner species; the sole exception is the very rare, almost extinct, lady's slipper orchid, which I am prepared to wager the Colonel had obtained from a florist.

For the Colonel was an amateur, and not a very enterprising one, either. In his foreword he naively confesses himself baffled by the ordinary flora, with its scientific classification of species; and in the subsequent text, invents a system of classification entirely his

Himantoglossum
Hircinum
Lizard Orchid
(Kent. June 1924.)

own. About the rarest orchids, which he had evidently not seen, his tone becomes almost sceptical; one feels that he doubts their very existence.

Poor Colonel Mackenzie! His book was not the best of introductions to its subject. Yet he was a true orchidomane, and I salute him across the years. I imagine him living in comfortable retirement in Surrey, in a red house with a drive and spiky gates, among pine trees; pottering on the downs above Betchworth and Shere, but not often venturing further afield. Probably he did possess a copy of Bentham and Hooker; but he could seldom have looked at it. It is a pleasing thought that another retired officer, Colonel Godfery, has since written the standard Monograph[1] on the British Orchidaceae. (He also lives in Surrey.)

So, with Colonel Mackenzie and Edward Step open before me, I addressed myself to the identification of Mr Bundock's new orchid (he had no name for it himself). Now, according to Colonel Mackenzie, the plant was none other than *Orchis militaris*, the military orchid. But according to Edward Step, it might equally well – more probably, in fact – be *Orchis purpurea*, the great brown-winged orchid, which the Colonel didn't even so much as mention. The discrepancy provoked in me a moral conflict; for I wanted, very badly, to find *Orchis militaris*.

The military orchid. . . . For some reason the name had captured my imagination. At this period – about 1916 – most little boys wanted to be soldiers, and I suppose I was no exception. The military orchid had taken on a kind of legendary quality, its image seemed fringed with the mysterious and exciting appurtenances of soldiering, its name was like a distant bugle call, thrilling and rather sad, a *cor au fond du bois*. The idea of a soldier, I think,

1. *Monograph and Iconograph of Native British Orchidaceae*, 1933.

had come to represent for me a whole complex of virtues which I knew that I lacked, yet wanted to possess: I was timid, a coward at games, terrified of the aggressively masculine, totemistic life of the boys at school; yet I secretly desired, above all things, to be like other people. These ideas had somehow become incarnated in *Orchis militaris.*

But alas! according to Edward Step, the military orchid occurred only in Oxfordshire, Berkshire, Buckinghamshire and Hertfordshire, and I lived in Kent. True, there was said to be a subspecies, *O. simia*, the monkey orchid, 'with narrower divisions of the crimson lip, occurring in the same counties as the type, with the addition of Kent'. But if Mr Bundock's orchid was not the military, still less could it be the monkey; its lip was not crimson, but, on the contrary, pale rose-coloured or nearly white, and spotted with purple. Moreover, the sepals and petals were striped and stippled with dark purplish-brown, which fitted with Step's description of *Orchis purpurea.* Furthermore, the great brown-winged orchid was said to grow in 'Kent and Sussex only'. Judging by Edward Step, Mr Bundock's orchid was, beyond the shadow of a doubt, *Orchis purpurea.*

And yet . . . and yet . . . if only it could be *Orchis militaris*! After all, if one could trust Colonel Mackenzie, it *was* the military. So far as he was concerned, there was no such thing as a great brown-winged orchid. All I had to do was to ignore Edward Step, and pin my faith to Colonel Mackenzie. The Colonel, moreover, provided an additional loophole for my conscience: in *his* description, there was no nonsense about Oxfordshire and Berkshire; he merely contented himself with saying that the plant was 'rare in spring', and grew 'in chalky districts only and not always there'. Consequently, since Kent was chalky, the military orchid might be expected to occur there. . . .

I repeated to myself the statements of each writer, till they sang in my mind like incantations. Rare in spring: in chalky districts only, and not always there. The words beckoned like a far bugle, remote and melancholy beyond mysterious hills. . . . Yes, it *must* be the military orchid. . . .

So Edward Step was firmly closed and put away, and I basked in the glory of having found (or at least been told where to find) the military orchid. Another book which was presented to me at this time – *British Wild Flowers*, by W. Graveson – confirmed my decision, the author relating how he had found the 'Military Orchis' in the Kentish woods. (No doubt, like Colonel Mackenzie, he considered O. *purpurea* to be the same as O. *militaris*.)

Conscience, however, triumphed in the end, and I had to admit that Mr Bundock's orchid was not the military but the great brown-winged. Edward Step, after all, could hardly have invented *Orchis purpurea* out of sheer malice. No, the military orchid, alas! was still unfound.

And it still is – at least by me, and, I imagine, for the last forty years, by anybody else. For *Orchis militaris* is one of several British plants which have mysteriously become extinct, or very nearly so. The last reliable record for it dates from 1902, when it was found in Oxfordshire. An unconfirmed report does, indeed, state that it occurred near Deal, in 1910. But botanists are sceptical about Kentish records for O. *militaris*; Edward Step, after all, was probably right. . . .

As for Colonel Mackenzie, I am prepared to bet that he had never seen either the military or the brown-winged – nor, for that matter, the 'subspecies known as the monkey orchid' which nowadays, raised to the status of a species, and more fortunate than its military relation, still survives in a single locality in Oxfordshire: the exact spot being a closely guarded secret, known only to a few botanists.

The Colonel, of course, was partly justified in his omission of the brown-winged and the monkey; his list of species, no doubt, was based on early editions of Bentham and Hooker, and consequently (more or less) on the original classification of Linnaeus, who 'lumped' O. *militaris*, *purpurea* and *simia* together as a single species. So I could have said, had I but known, that in identifying Mr Bundock's orchid as the military, I was merely following the example of Linnaeus. I am still, I must confess, in my less conscientious moments half-inclined to yield to the temptation.

II

NO PSYCHOANALYST, so far as I know, has yet attempted to explain the love of flowers in Freudian terms. Art has long since been reduced to its true status – a mere function of the neurotic personality; the young Mozart presents a perfectly clear clinical picture. Even the scientist can be explained away, I suppose, in Adlerian terms, as a victim of organic inferiority. But the botanophile – the unscientific lover of flowers, as opposed to the professional botanist – remains a mystery. It may be that his singular passion is a relic of totemism; flowers, perhaps, provide a lodgment for the External Soul, thereby rendering the body invulnerable against all perils, magical or otherwise. Doubtless, the matter will be cleared up before long; but – happily, perhaps, for its adherents – the cult of botanophily has been so far neglected by investigators.

Often, but not always, the botanophile is precocious. A family legend relates that, at the age of four, I could identify by name any or all of the coloured plates in Edward Step's *Wayside and*

Woodland Blossoms. For the truth of this I cannot vouch; but my
own memory testifies to the fact that I could perform this disgustingly
precocious feat two or three years later. By that time I had learnt to
read; and, not content with the English names, I memorised many
of the Latin and Greek ones as well. Some of these (at the age
of eight) I conceitedly incorporated into a school essay at the day
school in Folkestone which I attended. The headmaster read the
essay aloud to the school (no wonder I was unpopular); but this
flattering tribute was mitigated by his pronunciation of the names.
My knowledge of Latin had scarcely progressed beyond the present
indicative of *amo*; for flower names I had my own pronunciation,
and the headmaster's version of them came as a shock. I still utter
the specific name of the bee orchid – *apifera* – with a slight feeling
of flouting my own convictions. I realise, now, that the accent is on
the second syllable, but my own inclination would still put it on
the third.

Why, without any particular encouragement, should flowers,
rather than stamps, butterflies or birds' eggs, have become my
ruling passion? True, I flirted, throughout my childhood, with
butterflies, tame grass snakes, home-made fireworks; but flowers
were my first love and seem likely to be my last.

Here I had better confess (since this book is largely about
flowers) that, not only am I not a true botanist, but that even as
a botanophile I am a specialist in the worst sense. Whole tracts of
the subject leave me cold: certain families or genera frankly bore
me, and always will – the Chenopodiaceae, for example, or those
tedious *Hieracii*, or the chickweeds. Recently I went with a real
botanist to the Sandwich golf links, celebrated for a number of rare
plants; it was a chilly afternoon in spring, and no weather to dawdle
unless for a very good reason. My friend was in pursuit of a rare
chickweed – or one, at any rate, that was rare in Kent – and every

few yards would throw himself flat on his face and remain there, making minute comparisons, while the glacial sea wind penetrated my clothes and reduced me to a state of frozen irritability. I could almost realise, on this occasion, how boring botanists must be to non-botanists. Yet had the elusive chickweed been, say a rare or critical marsh orchid, I would have risked pneumonia with as much enthusiasm as my botanist friend. A rare broomrape – *Orobanche caryophyllacea* – was indeed said to grow half a mile away, and I was as anxious to see it as my friend was to identify his chickweed. Why? The broomrapes are not notably beautiful. The clove-scented one is very rare, certainly; but mere rarity is not enough – the chickweed was rare, too. If the love of flowers itself is hard to explain, still harder is it to account for the peculiar attraction of certain plants or groups of plants.

Most obvious, of course, is the appeal of the Orchidaceae. It is easy enough to see the attraction of those floral aristocrats, with their equivocal air of belonging partly to the vegetable, partly to the animal kingdom. I yielded to their seduction at an unnaturally early age. But broomrapes? Chickweeds? There seems no reasonable explanation.

For non-professionals, like myself, such prejudices condition the extent of such little true botanical knowledge as we may possess. I know something about the flower-structure of the orchids, because I happen to like them, and a minimum of technical knowledge is necessary to identify the more critical species. But ask me to explain by what similarities of internal structure a delphinium is placed in the same family as a buttercup, and I am stumped. Yet I like the Ranunculaceae. To find either of the two hellebores is always a major thrill – particularly *Helleborus faetidus*, the setterwort, that august and seldom haunter of a few south-country chalk hills. One of my cherished ambitions is to see the truly wild monkshood in the few places where it is still said to survive; and another is to find in England the wild larkspur which I have seen growing as a cornfield-weed in Italy. The Ranunculaceae, however, as a family, just fail to excite me sufficiently to overcome my ignorance about their internal affairs. I admire them as I once heard a certain French lady, at Cassis, confessing that she admired the proletariat: '*J'adore les ouvriers*,' she declared, '*mais de loin, de loin*.'

III

I SUPPOSE for many people, as for myself, some childhood scene tends to become archetypal, the hidden source of all one's private imagery, tinging the most banal and quotidian words and objects with its distinct yet often unrecognised flavour. For me the village where we spent my childhood summers, where Mr Bundock lurked like a wood spirit in the warm, tree-muffled evenings, has this quality of legend. Certain basic, ordinary words such as 'wood', 'stream', 'village', in whatever context I may use them, will always, for me, evoke a particular wood, a particular stream, almost always in the immediate neighbourhood of our summer cottage.

For some people, I suppose, such words have become entirely abstracted from any such archetypal images – mere generic names for natural features. One might divide the human race into those who develop this power of abstraction and those who don't; it would probably serve as well as a good many other artificial categories. I have read somewhere that the more primitive languages have no generic name for, say, a tree or a camel; each individual camel or tree has to be given a name of its own as required. Children, like other savages, develop the 'abstracting' faculty slowly; many, like myself, never fully develop it at all.

A word which, more than most, evokes for me that Kentish village, is the word 'afternoon'. The cool, green, slumberous syllables refuse to be detached from the cottage garden, drowsing among its trees, the tea table laid in the shade, the buzzing of wasps busy among the fallen plums – a subdued, perpetual bourdon orchestrating the shriller melodic line of birdsong and the voices of children. In memory, the village seems held in a perpetual trance of summer afternoons: possibly for no better reason than that we seldom visited it in the winter. Half-hidden by trees and (in those days) remote in its valley, the little street with its scattered houses, its squat-towered church and its slate-roofed Victorian pub was still comparatively 'undiscovered'. A celebrated Jacobean divine had ended his days in the rectory; in the closing years of my childhood, an eminent novelist inhabited the dower house, a pleasant early-nineteenth-century building near the church; these were the village's only claim to fame. But even in my earliest childhood the bourgeois invasion had begun – my family, indeed, formed part of the vanguard – and nowadays the number of cottages inhabited by land-workers is in a small minority. The lanes and hedges, today, have become scrupulously tidy; the grass in the churchyard is punctually cut; the cottages have sprouted new wings, carefully disguised by expensive 'weathered' tiles; the dower house is to be pulled down; and the eminent novelist is commemorated by a bogus-Tudor porch tacked on to the parish hall. The village, in fact, is fast becoming a garden suburb.

But it was not only words which were to become permanently associated with that particular childhood background. Whole tracts of experience – certain types of landscape, certain phrases and passages of music, innumerable smells, particular ways of speech became for me (and remained) imprinted indelibly with the same atmosphere of a summer afternoon. The process of identification began early: when my Nurse read Beatrix Potter aloud, and still more when I had learnt to read myself, the landscape of *Mr Tod* and *Jemima Puddleduck* seemed indistinguishable from the landscape of our village. I knew the track which Tommy Brock took through the wood, when he made off with the rabbit-babies: it was none other than the path, fringed with bluebells, through the copse which we called Teazel Wood. The hillside where Cottontail lived with her husband was the park behind the big Queen Anne manor house. . . . 'The sun was still warm and slanting on the hill-pastures' – how well I recognised the description! Tommy Brock's abduction of the baby rabbits, the agonised pursuit by Benjamin Bunny and Peter Rabbit – the whole long-drawn and tragic tale was for me bound up (and indeed still is) with a landscape which I knew and loved. Reason tells me, nowadays, that the scene of Beatrix Potter's stories was really Westmorland; nonetheless, the path through Teazel Wood is still haunted, for me, by Tommy Brock and the foxy-whiskered gentleman.

I have wondered, too, lately, why when rereading Ronald Firbank, I should so often be reminded of Miss Trumpett; and can only conclude that the peculiarly gushing, late-Edwardian conversational style which characterises so much of his dialogue (especially in *Vainglory*) is for me an echo of tea parties at the cottage where, like an exotic bird, plumed with crimson or scarlet, Miss Trumpett would suddenly appear and hold me spellbound by such a vision of sophisticated elegance as I had never beheld before in my life.

If Mr Bundock haunted the village evenings with his mops and buckets and disinfectants, it was Miss Trumpett who was the presiding genius of the afternoons. Teatime was her hour: I cannot believe that I ever saw her in the morning, though in the nature of things I must have done. Of Creole extraction, her mother had married a well-off English solicitor; the Trumpetts had, indeed, become more English than the royal family: their very Englishness was excessive, and served to enhance their innate exoticism.

Miss Trumpett, as I remember her, was (perhaps consciously) slightly Beardsley: full-lipped, with powdered cheeks of a peculiarly thick, granular texture, and raven-black frizzy hair. She affected clothes, too, which put the village in a flutter: on summer afternoons she would appear in gowns worthy of Ascot, and wearing an immense hat of crimson or vermilion, and scarlet shoes (like Oriane de Guermantes). A scarlet umbrella completed the ensemble; or, at other times, a parasol which I was assured in awed tones, was authentically 'Burmese'. (The idea of Burma is associated for me, to this day, with the curious 'tacky' texture and resinous smell of Miss Trumpett's parasol.) Her whole personality seemed to have a velvety bloom which, with her richly powdered cheeks, suggested to me an auricula. I was entirely fascinated; all the more so, since Miss Trumpett had a slight flavour of forbidden fruit.

Nothing very scandalous; but rumour (and something more than rumour) said that she had settled in the village to 'catch' a certain well-off bachelor who owned one of the two 'big' houses. Poor Miss Trumpett! She never caught her man; but she remained, for my Nurse, who strongly disapproved of her, 'that naughty Miss T'. Her naughtiness, I fancy, consisted chiefly in her clothes and her general air of 'smartness'; she was, ever so slightly, 'fast'. I should conjecture that she was, in fact, completely virtuous; she was certainly extremely conventional in her tastes, with a passion for bridge which was sometimes indulged in the company of my parents (for the most modest of points – she would never have consented, any more than Mrs Hurstpierpoint in *Valmouth*, to play for '*immodest*' ones).

No, there was nothing very 'naughty' about Miss Trumpett; but the word, with its tang of Edwardian gaieties, is fitting enough. She was my first contact with the exotic: her clothes, her Latin American ancestry, her putative wickedness, contributed something to the effect she had upon me; but what I remember chiefly is her voice – rich, resonant, with the same velvety, powdery texture as her outward appearance. Her conversation was enlivened with the argot (already rather dated at this period) of Edwardian chic. Phrases like 'too divine' or 'divvy' – unknown in my family circle – fell on my ears with an effect of alien and slightly immoral elegance. She would speak slightingly of something or somebody as 'very *mere*'. Once, at tea, when I announced that I was 'full', she pulled me up sharply: it was rude to say that, she told me. If I *must* announce the fact, I ought to say, '*Je suis rempli*'. She was free with her French phrases; and this, my first contact with the language, was to confer upon it, for all time, a certain imprint of exoticism, something of the elegant, powdered, auricula-like quality of Miss Trumpett herself.

She was a great reader; in her cottage were ranged (among palms and fire-screens and unseasonable flowers) the complete works of Meredith; a little later it was Henry James; later still, Galsworthy. She played the piano, too, and sang: rattling off *The Vision of Salome* or some new and fashionable tango with great spirit, or singing *Every Morn I Bring Thee Violets* or *Sweetest Li'l Feller* in a voice which invested the songs with an air of mondain luxury and splendour, an atmosphere of plush, mimosa and the Edwardian jollifications of Homburg or Monte Carlo.

One night, greatly daring, I walked round the garden with her by moonlight: it was my first romantic encounter. Had it been the Jersey Lily herself or la Belle Otéro I could not have been more thrilled. I paid for the experience in the acute embarrassment

Orchis   Purpurea
Lady   Orchid
(Kent : May . 1940.)

which I suffered on returning to my Nurse. Contemptuous, she said nothing; but her disapproval was all too obvious. . . . I did not repeat the exploit. Obscurely, perhaps, I felt that I wasn't cut out for such as Miss Trumpett; her world was too alien, too romantically remote.

Nor, it seemed, was I cut out for her young nephew and niece who, with their parents, took a cottage in the village that summer or the next. They were pretty and well-behaved children, excessively polite and even more conventional than their aunt. I loathed them. In vain did our respective parents seek to engineer an alliance: I would have none of it. In the company of the little Trumpetts I became more shy, more ill-behaved and in general more unpleasant than I was by nature. I preferred the children of a local farmer, Mr Igglesden; they were, indeed, my only friends, and I was happy with them. The little Trumpetts showed no inclination (fortunately for me) to fraternise with the Igglesdens; so I was able, in time, to avoid the bourgeoisie entirely and to throw in my lot with the working class. This phase in my political evolution was speeded up considerably when, at one of my unavoidable encounters with the Trumpett children, their mother overheard me explaining to Mary Trumpett the difference between a male and female tiger moth. Thenceforth I was considered a corrupt influence, and encouraged no further.

But before the final split, the Trumpetts did prove of some value after all. One evening, coming back from a picnic in the woods, they showed me an unusual flower they had found. It was a year or two since Mr Bundock had brought me the orchid which had provoked in me such an acute moral conflict; moreover, I had never managed to find it for myself. Now, in the plant found by the little Trumpetts, I recognised Mr Bundock's mysterious orchid. This time, I received exact directions about the locality; and shortly afterwards, in a copse only half a mile from the village, I was able to find it for myself. It was not the military orchid – I had long ago, reluctantly, abandoned that idea, in spite of Colonel Mackenzie. But it *was* the great brown-winged – or, as it is more pleasantly called, the lady orchid; the most regal of British orchids, and perhaps the loveliest of English wild flowers: its tall pagodas of brown-hooded, white-lipped blossoms towering grandly, like some alien visitor, exotic as Miss Trumpett at a village tea party, above the fading bluebells and the drab thickets of dog's mercury, in a wood which I had known all my childhood, but whose distinguished inhabitant I had never before discovered.

IV

IF THE VILLAGE of our summer holidays was an afternoon-land, tranced in a perpetual and postprandial drowsiness, our real home, at Sandgate, was by contrast matutinal: my memories of it are bathed in the keen, windy light of spring mornings, a seaside gaiety and brilliance haunted by the thud of waves on the shingle and the tang of seaweed. At the time, Sandgate lacked romance, being merely the place where we lived (my father had his business in the neighbouring town of Folkestone); during the autumn and winter, the village became for me a Land of Lost Content, the symbol of a happiness which would only be renewed again in the spring. (With most children, this state of affairs is reversed: it is the seaside which enshrines the memory of summer-happiness, not, as for me, the country.) Later, in adolescence, Sandgate too would become part of the legend of the past, the private myth; but in childhood, it was the

village in the Elham Valley which, alone, possessed the quality of
romance. When I began to write, at about fifteen, I naturally turned
to the valley village for the background of my stories. But that
country legend had, after all, grown up with me; from earliest days
I had surrounded the valley landscape with an aura of sentimental
nostalgia, and in consequence, my adolescent recollections of it
were apt to seem rather second-hand – mere memories of memories;
my attempts to write about it seemed over-stylised and at the same
time too facile. Some small episode, trivial as Proust's madeleine-
dipped-in-tea, must have accidentally evoked Sandgate for me at
about that time, and the whole atmosphere and flavour of our
seaside home was recalled as Combray was for Proust: vivid and
immediate, springing nakedly from the past without the swaddling
of conscious sentimentality which had obscured my recollections of
our country village.

Our house was on the Undercliff: behind it, the cliff rose steeply
to the Folkestone Leas; below, a garden descended in terraces to
the beach. The house, from the road, presented an undistinguished
facade of grey cement; at the back, however (on the seaward-facing
side), it was faced with white stucco, and the windows were fitted
with green shutters, giving to the house an oddly Mediterranean air.
The tamarisks in the garden (and an occasional stone pine) added to
this illusion of meridional gaiety. Had I but known it, the rest of the
flora, too, provided curious parallels with that of the Mediterranean
seaboard. Stationed at Ancona during the Second World War, I was
repeatedly struck by the number of plants which I remembered as
growing at Sandgate: horned poppy, bristly oxtongue, tree mallow,
henbane. (The maritime flora is, in fact, singularly uniform from
northern to southern Europe.) Walking on the cliffs by the Adriatic,
I might have fancied myself back at Sandgate: till the scattered stars

of pink anemones, or a glimpse of an outlying cornfield carpeted with wild red tulips, recalled me to a sense of reality.

One summer – I think it was 1916 – a miracle occurred: the cliffs above our house were carpeted, in July, with the brilliant blue spikes of viper's bugloss. The plant was common enough on the cliffs, but had never occurred in anything like such quantity: nor has it ever done so since. The other day, travelling up by the Portsmouth line from Petersfield, I saw near Liphook, for only the second time in my life, the miracle repeated: a field covered, as thickly as if with bluebells, by that noble and stately flower. The blue is of a brighter shade than that of bluebells: in the July sun it seems positively to sizzle and splutter, like a blue Bengal light.

I know of no reason for these occasional displays by the bugloss: they appear to be as irregular and unpredictable as (in southern latitudes) the aurora borealis. But the year 1916 was, I suspect, something of an *annus mirabilis* for botanists; or do I imagine so merely because I myself was lucky? Henbane was one of my finds that year: not a great rarity, but often appearing sporadically, and disappearing again completely from the locality for a period of years. Its creamy flowers, veined with purple, and the clammy, corpse-like texture of its leaves, impressed me at the time with an agreeable sense of Evil. The mandrake itself is a fairly harmless-looking plant; it is a pity that the name, with all its satanic associations, cannot be transferred to the henbane. (Is henbane the 'hebanon' of *Hamlet*? Nobody seems to know.) In practice, if not in theory, flower names are oddly interchangeable. Many non-botanists, for instance, are convinced that they know the deadly nightshade when they see it; but in nine cases out of ten, the plant they are thinking of proves to be the woody nightshade, or bittersweet. It is useless to tell them that the woody nightshade, that first cousin of the potato, is not only not deadly, but scarcely even poisonous at all: they are convinced that it is lethal, and if shown the true deadly nightshade, a rare-ish plant of southern chalk downland, will refuse to believe you. It is a mistake that never fails to irritate me, detracting as it does from the sinister dignity of a plant which has a good claim to be the chief villain of the British flora: a plant 'so furious and deadly' (as Gerard remarks) that it is just as well it is not commoner than it is.

Another 'find' of 1916 was the coltsfoot: it seems incredible that I had not found it before. But I had formed the mistaken idea that it was a rarity, and therefore, presumably by a kind of inverted wishful thinking, was simply unable to see it. The mistake arose through a misreading of Edward Step's account of the plant, which refers to a dubious variety recorded by the Scottish botanist George Don, from 'the high mountains of Clova'. This statement was taken, by me, to refer to the common coltsfoot; and doubtless because of the romantic sound of the 'high mountains of Clova', I conceived a passion for the plant. I dreamt of coltsfoot, I insisted on my Nurse purchasing some coltsfoot rock at a chemist's, I copied Edward Step's plate of it in washy watercolours.

Then one day a teacher at my first day school happened to mention that it grew on the foreshore at Seabrook, near Sandgate. On a March morning I set out to look for it: not really believing that a plant hailing from the 'high mountains of Clova' could grow half a mile from my own door. But there, on the shingle flats by the beginning of the Hythe Military Canal – there, no more than a stone's throw from the sea, in a spot I must have passed a dozen times before – there was the coltsfoot, its golden ruffs widespread in the morning sun, abundant as any dandelion; and perfectly at home. I was delighted; the discovery made me happy for weeks afterwards. But somehow, after that, the coltsfoot lost some of its romance. Like a new and unusual word, encountered for the first

time, which one is sure to meet again within a day or two, I soon
began to see the coltsfoot everywhere.

Yet coltsfoot has not, even today, entirely lost the romantic
aura with which I at one time invested it. Seeing it from a train,
precociously ablaze on some chalky embankment, or even straying
up the sidings to the edge of some suburban platform, I still find
myself cherishing a superstitious belief that the seeds must have
blown there from the romantic heights of Clova.

I have never been to Clova: I don't even know where it is. For me
it belongs in the same category as the Zemmery Fidd and the Great
Gromboolian Plain. Similarly, I am inclined to be sceptical about the
existence of Mayo and Galway. Here I think Colonel Mackenzie is
to blame again; for those romantic-sounding counties were for me
merely the home of *Habenaria intacta*, or, as it is called nowadays,
Neotinea intacta, the dense-flowered orchid. Unlike the coltsfoot,
Neotinea preserved its romantic aloofness, and refused to oblige
me by occurring at Sandgate. But having found the mysterious
denizen of Clova almost, so to speak, at my backdoor, I saw no
reason why the Entire Habenaria (thus it was crudely Englished)
should not turn up too.

I lived in hopes: the 'Habenaria' shared some of the glamour
of *Orchis militaris*. It must have been in the year 1916 that Mr
Bundock brought me the lady orchid; and it was in 1916, too, I am
almost sure, that I was first taken to The Hills.

They were referred to as 'The Hills' – those low downs behind
Folkestone, knobbly and broken in outline by barrows and
earthworks – rather as dwellers in the plains of India speak of
Shimla, though not (at least by my family) with any desire to visit
them. Indeed, my mother insisted that they were 'very dull', and the
long-promised expedition to Sugarloaf or Caesar's Camp was for

one reason or another delayed from year to year. Our walks took
us almost to the foot of them: they loomed grey and austere against
the sky, ringed with their concentric terraces trodden by grazing
cattle. Beyond them lay The Country – a country which, in fact,
I knew, but which, cut off by that high, forbidden barrier, seemed
immensely romantic and mysterious.

At last I heard from somebody that the bee orchid grew on
Sugarloaf. I refused to be baulked any longer, and one June
morning we set off: taking the scarlet East Kent bus from Coolinge
Lane, traversing the Sandgate Road and the mean streets beyond
the town hall, till at last we began to climb the Canterbury hill.
The bus dropped us at the Black Bull – a pub which in those days
marked the fringes of the town. A sign hung from it, inscribed with
the magical words 'Nalder and Collyer's Entire'. Entire what? I
still don't know. The adjective seemed to flap, mysteriously, in
the air, demanding its appropriate substantive. I soon supplied
one. Nalder and Collyer's became linked, for me, with *Habenaria
intacta*, the Entire Habenaria. The Black Bull sign seemed a good
omen. (Alas! the Black Bull, today, is 'Entire' no more, and the
sign, unromantically, announces the ownership of Messrs. Ind,
Coope and Allsopp.)

We walked up the hill through the hot June morning, the air
heavy with chalk dust and petrol. Just beyond the Black Bull, a
farm with a thatched barn and outhouses huddled among the raw
new villas, its smell of dung bravely combating the town smells –
the stink of petrol, dust, pubs; an outpost of the country overtaken
and nearly submerged by the licking tentacles of suburb. We left
the main road by the track skirting the foot of the hills: there was
a sudden muffling of traffic noises, a country silence murmurous
with the hum of bees and the scraping of grasshoppers. We crossed
a field, climbed a stile, and entered the Promised Land at last – the

Ophrys
Arachnites
Late Spider Orchid.
(Kent. June 1939.)

Ophrys
Apifera
Bee Orchid

Ophrys
Trollii
Wasp Orchid
(Glos. July 1946.)

mysterious, hitherto-forbidden land of The Hills.

Against the hot blue sky, the terraced knoll loomed enormous, its summit lost in a shimmering heat-haze. The grassy flanks seemed to radiate a reflected heat, enfolding us in a weighted, thyme-scented silence, enhanced rather than disturbed by the monotone of a thousand insects. On the banks at the hill's foot, the cropped turf was gemmed with the small downland flowers, many of which I had never seen before: rockrose, milkwort, centaury. In that moment, I encountered a new Love – the chalkdown flora: a Love to which I have always remained faithful. Most botanists have their ecological preferences; and though I have had brief spells of infidelity with peat bogs, with sand dunes or even with wealden clay, the downs remain my Cynara, and I still return to them with some of the pristine delight of that first visit to The Hills.

A miniature chalkpit dazzled our eyes a little way up the hill. Running ahead, I paused near the edge of it: a plant had caught my eye, a flower with pink petals on which a bee seemed to be resting. Suddenly I realised that this was the goal of our pilgrimage; like Langhorne,

> I sought the living bee to find
> And found the picture of a bee.

Yes, there was no doubt of it: a single plant, standing stiff and aloof, bearing proudly aloft its extraordinary insect-flowers, like archaic jewels rifled from some tomb; I had found the bee orchid.

As it happened, I added, that day, a greater rarity to my collection than I suspected. True, I had found the bee orchid, which was exciting enough. But years later, looking through pressed specimens of 'bee orchids' labelled 'Sugarloaf, 1916', some of them proved, beyond a doubt, to be not the bee orchid at all, but the late spider (*Ophrys arachnites*) – one of the rarest of British orchids, confined to a few localities in East Kent. Like the lady, the late spider was not even mentioned by Colonel Mackenzie; Edward Step did refer to it, in passing, as a 'subspecies', but I was bored by such hairsplitting. To have found the bee orchid was good enough for me.

The late spider orchid, nowadays, is of course considered a 'good' species; but it has, unfortunately, become much more rare. It resembles the bee orchid, but has a fuller, more swollen lip, and the 'sting' (supposing a spider to have a sting) projects forward, instead of being recurved, as in the bee. It was not surprising that I failed to recognise it: I have known botanists who have lived near the late spider localities all their lives, and yet are unable to distinguish the two species.

Another insect orchid was said to haunt the Folkestone hills – the drone orchid, a variety of the early spider; I must have first read about it in one or another of the works of Anne Pratt. I found the early spider in due course, but the drone eluded me. No wonder: for it is no longer 'accepted' by most botanists as a good variety and is probably a myth.

How many people, nowadays, remember Anne Pratt? She is hardly to be included among the 'classical' botanists; yet, if less illustrious than Brown, Babington, Hooker and other of her contemporaries, she scarcely deserves the oblivion into which she seems to have fallen. So far as I know, no memoir of her exists; one still comes across her works in second-hand bookshops, but they must all have been long out of print. Her magnum opus in four volumes, *Flowering Plants, Grasses, Sedges and Ferns of Great Britain*, is certainly somewhat out of date from a strictly botanical point of view. But it is still an excellent bedside book. It is leisurely and discursive; the botanical literature of several centuries is ransacked for titbits of plant-lore; there are innumerable excursions, often extremely entertaining, into folklore, herbal medicine and so on. Nor are the Arts forgotten: the verses quoted, in praise of or in connection with plants would, if collected, form an instructive anthology, not only of botanical verse, but of forgotten minor verse in general. Bishop Mant (who was he?) is perhaps the most often quoted; but many of the poems were written, so the author tells us, 'especially for this work'.

Erudite and allusive as she is, however, it is in her more personal moments that Miss Pratt is at her best. Hearing, for instance, that 'the root of our native catmint, if chewed, will make the most gentle persons fierce and wrathful', she decides, with a commendable scientific curiosity, to verify the statement. 'The writer of these pages, who, with a friend who joined in the experiment, chewed a piece of this bitter and aromatic substance, of the length of a finger, is able . . . to assure her readers that for at least four-and-twenty hours after taking it, both she and her companion retained a perfect equanimity of temper and feeling.'

It would have taken more than catmint, one feels, to impair the equanimity of Miss Pratt. One pictures her as middle-aged, sensible and humorous, immensely energetic, and quite undaunted by the weather, gamekeepers, spiked fences and other such obstacles to the pursuit of her profession. From internal evidence, it appears that she lived at or near Dover: there are innumerable references to the flora of the Dover Cliffs, and a number of the plants she mentions as growing there can still be found in the same locality – for example, the wild cabbage and Nottingham catchfly. (Others, such as the dwarf orchid, have alas! become rare since her day.)

Miss Pratt, in fact, emerges as a glorified (and professionalised) version of a type: the Victorian lady-botanist. She was more

Ophrys Aranifera
Early Spider Orchid
(Kent. May 1939)

Ophrys Aranifera
Early Spider Orchid
(Kent. May. 1939.)

Ophrys Muscifera : Fly Orchid.
(Kent. June 1939.)

industrious, more energetic than most, and turned her knowledge to professional use; but she remains an amateur, nonetheless: a cultivated lady of the period, with an eminently suitable and 'educational' hobby.

Her book has a special charm for those who, like myself, have a taste for odd and mainly useless scraps of information. It is pleasant, for instance, to learn that Antonius Musa, physician to the Emperor Augustus, 'wrote a whole book setting forth the excellences of Betony, which he said would cure forty-seven disorders'; or, of the Roman nettle, that Julius Caesar's legionaries, 'having heard much of the coldness of our climate, thought it was not to be endured without some friction that might warm their blood; they therefore used this nettle to warm and chafe their benumbed limbs.' And again, of the ordinary nettle (not the Roman one): 'We have ourselves in childhood often supped off a dish of nettle-tops boiled for about twenty minutes and eaten with salt and vinegar.' The author remarks that they 'seemed delicious', but cautiously adds that 'their flavour may have been improved by the fact of their having been gathered during a long country walk, and by our having watched them during the process of cooking.'

Miss Pratt is a great one for local nomenclature; and, not content with English names, she more often than not supplies half a dozen foreign ones as well. Thus herb Paris, she tells us, is in France called *parisette* (a name which somehow suggests Mistinguett and the old Moulin Rouge), *raisin de renard* and *étrangle loup*; in Germany it is *Einbeere*, and in Italy *uva di volpe*. Of the sun spurge, she remarks that the old herbalists called it sun tithymale, while the Dutch name for it is *wolfenmilch*; and in England it is known variously as churnstaff, wartweed, cat's milk, wolf's milk and littlegood.

Here is a specimen of the occasional verse 'written for our volume' – in this case by Calder Campbell:

> October winds were drifting yellow leaves
> From wintering trees – October waves rose high
> Against the barren shores of Calais, where
> I stood and mark'd the stormy sea that frown'd
> 'Neath frowning skies. 'Is there no hope?' quoth I . . .

And so on for a further twenty-eight lines, in which the poet's melancholy is finally cheered by the discovery of the sea buckthorn.

One would like, too, to try some of Miss Pratt's less-familiar herbal beverages – for instance, wild marjoram tea, which she tells us 'is very grateful and refreshing, and doubtless is wholesome, though its efficacy in preserving health may be somewhat overrated by country people'. Less successful, among her experiments in country recipes, was the use of the lesser celandine as a vegetable. The leaves, she tells us, were 'formerly boiled and eaten; but the author, who has tried their worth, cannot say much in their favour'.

But if Miss Pratt was prepared to experiment with the gastronomic uses of plants, her attitude to the darker side of plant lore was one of rational but pious scepticism. Quoting Ben Jonson's *Witches' Song*, in connection with the horned poppy, she cannot resist a slightly complacent reference to the decline of superstition. 'The light of Revelation,' (she writes) 'which has dawned now on every British village, and brought its teachings to hall and cottage, has dispelled fancies and practices which were sanctioned in other times, and none dream now of gathering the poppy for incantations.'

Pious, cultivated, sensible, immensely energetic – one would like to have known Miss Pratt. One imagines her setting forth, on some summer's afternoon in the 1850s, perhaps escorted by some frock-coated clergyman, or by the friend who shared in the catmint experiment, sensibly clad, minutely observant, humorously deprecating the vestiges of superstition among the villagers, and always ready, by an appropriate word here or there, to assist in spreading the Light of Revelation. Toiling over the Dover Cliffs for *Silene nutans*, wading through the marshes about Sandwich for the greater spearwort, or searching 'in the woodlands or on the bushy hill' for *Orchis purpurea* – one sees her, indomitable but incurably ladylike, pursuing her purposeful way through the Kentish countryside, her tweeded figure bathed in the warm, golden light of a Victorian Sunday afternoon in summer. One almost feels that, like the Scholar Gipsy, she may yet haunt, at sunset, the hillsides of Kearsney and Alkham, behind Dover, or those remoter woodlands about Nonington or Womenswold; laden, no doubt, with a 'store of flowers':

> the frail-leaf'd white anemone,
> Dark bluebells drench'd with dews of summer eves,
> And purple orchises with spotted leaves . . .

Or possibly some rare fern or rush, or herb Paris or hemp agrimony which is called in Russia *griwa kouskaja*, or marjoram to brew a 'grateful and refreshing' tea. And it is not improbable, either, that

> Far on the forest-skirts, where none pursue,
> On some mild pastoral slope . . .

she may have stumbled, quite accidentally, in the darkening shade, upon the military orchid itself.

V

IF IT WAS an *annus mirabilis* for botany, 1916 was also, for me, the end of a Golden Age; for in this year I started to go to school. It was the beginning of a process which was to last nearly twelve years, during which I certainly suffered more acutely than I ever have since. The best thing one can say, I suppose, for the (bourgeois) English educational system is that it immunises one to a great extent against subsequent horrors. I had cause to be grateful for it, at least, in the army, where one saw the State-educated soldier, uprooted from the home environment for the first time in his life, suffering all the torments of homesickness which I had endured – and more or less come to terms with – at the age of eleven.

My initiation into school life, however, in 1916, was sufficiently mild: I was not sent to a boarding school, but merely to a kindergarten attached to a large and flourishing local girls' school, called Gaudeamus. This, moreover, I attended only in the mornings; so that Gaudeamus, for me, exists in memory as a morning-world, its rooms bathed perpetually in the early sunlight. I cannot imagine what it looked like in the afternoon: I am inclined to think that, like E.M. Forster's cow, it simply wasn't there.

The school stood beneath the cliffs, and the garden and playground, fringed with glaucous, billowing tamarisks, abutted on the beach. Within, the rooms seemed enormous, their high windows and polished floors reflecting the morning glare of sunlight, and echoing perpetually with the thud and hiss of the waves on the shingle.

Gaudeamus, as its name implied, inculcated a breezy and strenuous optimism. Miss Pinecoffin, its founder, had 'advanced' ideas, and had even been heard to speak in favour of co-education; but there was nothing revolutionary about Gaudeamus, and co-education was confined to the kindergarten. The girls might wear djibbahs, but there was no nonsense about Montessori or the Laboratory system: their education was soundly based on the School Certificate, the Higher Local and the Church of England. With such a firm basis of orthodoxy, Miss Pinecoffin could afford to spread herself a little in the matter of environment; and the interior decoration of Gaudeamus represented all that was most respectably artistic and 'progressive' at the turn of the century. Corot and Greuze hung on the walls, and Rossetti's *Beata Beatrix* in muddy monochrome; in the green-tiled fireplaces stood bulging jars of beaten copper, filled, in summer, with yellow flags or foxgloves. The singular flora of art nouveau – sprawling water lilies and fleurs-de-lis – burgeoned unexpectedly in corners; the chairs were all of an exceedingly uncomfortable, neo-Morrissy pattern, with high backs bored, in the centre, with curious heart-shaped holes. The heavy oak doorways (opening by means of enormous and cumbrous wooden latches) were provided with latticed panels of thick green glass. The rooms seemed always cold; yet, despite the supplies of fresh air, a faint but characteristic odour haunted their draughty spaces: a mingled taint of floor polish, dried ink and yesterday's meals.

It was all very inspiriting and healthy. Perpetually, it seemed, little girls in sage-green djibbahs were tearing breathlessly to and fro, as though the school were run on the lines of a military detention barracks, where all orders are carried out at the double. I was terrified: the tempo was too fast for me, and my hours in the kindergarten were spent mainly in unlearning, in a daze of unfamiliar words and objects, all I had learnt in the nursery.

Miss Prendergast, who taught in the kindergarten, was kind but rather overwhelming. When she kissed me on the first morning, her hair smelt of dandruff. I detested being kissed, anyway, but worse was in store. The French mademoiselle, by way of enlivening her French classes, insisted on playing kiss-in-the-ring. When my turn came, I firmly refused to be kissed. Threats, persuasions, appeals to my vanity – all proved useless. I remained mutely but firmly rebellious. Finally it was decided that I should be allowed to shake hands instead of kissing. The fact of being made an exception increased my agonies tenfold; nonetheless, I had won my point.

Sometimes Miss Prendergast took us for a botany ramble. (It was she who had destroyed my illusions about the coltsfoot.) I should have liked these rambles, but my pleasure in them was entirely destroyed by a paralysing fear that we might encounter some member of my family. Within the bounds of the school itself, I was prepared to suffer any amount of indignity or humiliation; I had already learnt to expect it. What I dreaded was that my family should be witnesses of my shame. Even at home, when visitors came to the house, I was overcome by an appalling self-consciousness; my every word and movement became automatically awkward and ridiculous, and I was tortured by the thought that my family were silently laughing at me. To have been seen, by my mother, on a botany ramble, seemed to me the lowest pitch of degradation. I tried to hide myself as much as possible behind the other children; I even had the courage to suggest a route which would take us as far as possible from our home. Mercifully we never did pass it; nor did we ever meet any member of the household. Once we had covered what I hoped was a safe distance from the house, my self-consciousness left me, and I was able to surprise Miss Prendergast by my precocious knowledge of botany. It was my first success: and her flattering comments did much to assuage the agonies of that first term at school.

In my memory the image of Miss Prendergast is wreathed about
with that squalid and uninteresting weed *Lepidium draba*. It was
Miss Prendergast who told me its English name – pepperwort. An
alien, introduced into Kent comparatively recently, it has spread
further inland, nowadays: and seeing its dirty white tufts in some
railway cutting, I am transported immediately to the high, empty,
sunlit rooms of Gaudeamus; I hear again the thin adolescent voices
chanting the daily psalm at Morning Prayers; the smell of floor
polish and seaweed is in my nostrils; and I see again the tall, wide-
flung windows giving upon the shingle playground, the hedges of
tamarisk and the pale-blue summer sea.

I was more interested, at that time, in flowers than in people.
Indeed, except in particular cases, I still am. Yet the social flora of
the Sandgate Undercliff, where we lived, was perhaps worthy of
study. I devoted to it approximately the same amount of attention
as I did to bird life – a subject which I found less interesting than
flowers or butterflies, but not without a certain attraction.

It was seldom, in the social milieu frequented by my family,
that I encountered anything so exotic and orchidaceous as Miss
Trumpett. Nonetheless, some of our neighbours might have been
described in the language of the floras as 'local', if not, 'very rare'.
Occasionally a true 'exotic', an 'adventive' species would make
its appearance, as when a certain Maharajah, with his suite, took
one of the neighbouring houses for a few months. Like some
Himalayan cistus or saxifrage escaped from a garden, he enlivened,
for a whole summer, the sedate paths of the Undercliff. Then (an
indigenous but distinctly flamboyant species) there was Mrs Croker,
the Anglo-Indian novelist, who sometimes came to tea with my
mother. And – better known to myself – there was the portentous
figure of Sessquire: tall, snowy-haired, with a monocle, he was a

Orchis
Praetermissa

Common Marsh Orchid

S.B.   S.B.

figure straight out of a Du Maurier drawing. Peering into my pram (or mail-cart), and booming a greeting in a voice which had once held London audiences spellbound, he seemed to me like some tall and very robust species of cotton grass, with his white bush of hair, and his mysterious, sibilant name which seemed to rustle like dried stalks in the wind. . . . One day my sister, turning a corner on one of the cliff paths, encountered Sessquire, inadequately concealed by a bush, obeying an importunate call of nature. Much tact was shown on both sides, but the episode doubtless left its mark; for me it has acquired a slight period interest, now that I realise that Sessquire's real name was Sir Squire Bancroft.

Eriophoroid, too, was 'Salvation' Hall, an ex-evangelical preacher with an immense white beard. He was also a botanist, and used to bicycle for miles in search of specimens. Once he showed me a pocketful of thrift, which he said he had gathered on Romney marsh. It was a plant I had never found, and perhaps I showed myself over-interested. At all events, he didn't offer me a specimen; remarking, with a cackle of laughter, as he remounted his bicycle, that when I was grown-up I should be able to go out to Romney marsh and get some too. It was pleasant, after that, to discover that thrift grew abundantly on the cliffs above our house; I can only hope that 'Salvation' Hall never discovered it.

Few grown-ups realise how subtly insulting their assumptions of superiority can be to a child. Indeed, one suffers more in childhood from wounded vanity than ever in later life. Once, I remember – I had left Gaudeamus, and gone to a day school in Folkestone – I returned from a school botany ramble with a bunch of woodland flowers: bluebells, wood spurge, weasel's snout, bugle. A lady – she must have been a parent visiting the school – professed a gushing interest in what I had found, and proceeded to ask me the name of each plant. All went well till I came to bugle.

'Bugloss,' she corrected me.

'Bugle,' I insisted.

'No, no. You mean *bugloss*, dear.'

'But I don't. It's *bugle*.'

'Bugloss,' she corrected me.

The lady began to look cross.

'Bugloss,' she repeated.

'Bugle,' I retorted, impenitently.

We parted unamicably: doubtless she thought I was a rude child. But I happened to be right, and she wrong. My plant was bugle. I could have probably told her the Latin name – *Ajuga reptans*. Yet I was helpless, I had no redress. She was a grown-up, and must therefore know better than I.

It is perhaps worth putting on record, for the benefit of the curious social historian, that when my family first went to live on the Undercliff, they were socially ostracised. A stigma attached to them only less black than that associated, in those days, with divorcées, inverts and card-sharpers. At tea parties, when the question arose whether my mother should be 'called on', it was whispered that my father was *in trade*. That, of course, settled it. One wasn't a snob, of course, but . . . well, there it was.

There it was: the dreadful truth was out. My father was 'in trade'. True, he was a wine merchant, and one's wine merchant even in those days ranked only a little below one's solicitor. If he had confined himself to having an office in London, he might have enjoyed the glorious privilege of being 'accepted' by the Undercliff. But alas! he actually had a *shop*. There it was, as large as life, in the Sandgate Road, Folkestone. True, it looked more like a bank, and was always called the 'Office'; but the fact remained, you could go into it and buy a bottle of wine (or even, for that matter, a bottle of beer) over the counter.

In later years the ban was apparently lifted: whether because our neighbours became less snobbish, or because they feared that my father, provoked beyond endurance, would put arsenic in their wine, I have no idea. The shadow remained in the background, at any rate: for when I first went, as a day boy, to a Folkestone preparatory school, I remember being haunted by a feeling of shame.

One day, at about this time, I was leaning out of the window with my brother, watching a column of soldiers marching past on their way to Folkestone Harbour, to embark for France. My brother asked me if I would like to be a soldier. I said I would. 'But of course,' he assured me, 'if you were in the army, you wouldn't be just one of those Tommies. You'd be an officer.'

This prophecy, at least, was not to be fulfilled; when I did join the army, twenty-four years later, I joined as a private, and remained one: a circumstance which would doubtless have prevented me from being 'called-on' by the Undercliff – supposing I had still lived there, or that there had been anybody else left to 'call'. Alas! the social ecology of Sandgate must have changed out of recognition, these many years; and the indigenous 'rarities' of my childhood have no doubt been long swept away by a weedy overgrowth amid which my own so-bourgeois family, had they remained there, might have enjoyed the prestige of a colony of orchids (or, shall I say, ranunculi?) surviving among a thicket of docks and nettles.

VI

Les seuls vrais paradis, said Proust, *sont les paradis qu'on a perdus*: and conversely, the only genuine Infernos, perhaps, are those which are yet to come. After the post-Munich period, with its atmosphere of slowly gathering crisis, the outbreak of war itself was like a sudden holiday, bringing a sense of release, almost of relief: the kind of relief which an invalid feels when a definite disease has declared itself, replacing the vague, indefinable malaise by a set of recognisable physical symptoms.

I remember, chiefly, at the time of Munich, rereading Beatrix Potter and Ronald Firbank; or playing the piano music of Erik Satie – cool and impersonal as plainchant. In those small and civil duchies one could forget, temporarily, the expanding suburbs of the mad capital, the smooth, ribbon-developed *Autobahnen* to the lands of violence and darkness. Or when these failed, there was the stoic's pleasure in occupations at once scholarly and useless: in my own case, writing a paper – with a rather conscious pedantry – on the distribution of *Orchis simia*, for the *Journal of Botany*; assuming, rather jauntily, the pose of the detached, the touch-line observer – an ostrich-defensiveness, like Housman with his footnotes to Manilius.

And lying awake in the small hours of those hot, rainy nights, hearing a plane drone overhead like the muttered presage of disaster, one's mind leapt to a sudden, annihilating consciousness of the future; the weak guts responded with a colic spasm, the ignominious grip of fear; and the feeling was suddenly oddly familiar, there was the sense of a duplicated experience reaching back to the remotest past. Where had one felt precisely this sensation before? And then the vision came of a corner-seat in a train, hard-boiled eggs, the *Strand Magazine*; the journey to a new school at the end of the summer holidays.

And one realised that the war would be like this: like the end of the holidays, going back to the red, unfriendly house with its laurelled drive and empty, polished rooms, smelling of ink and varnish, loud with jokes about bums and farts. Wake up, brace up, be keen, put your back into it: school is the world in miniature, Life is a football match . . . The hearty games master showing off his muscles in the changing room – 'Gosh, Sir, you must be awfully strong' – and the smell of the bogs: locking oneself in to indulge the nostalgic tears, living only for the holidays.

Yes, the war would be like this. But at this school, of course, the holidays might never come . . .

Thank goodness none of it was true. Life is not like a football match, even in wartime: the war was certainly uncomfortable, but not to be compared with the horrors of an English prep school. And for me, happening to be lucky, the holidays have come again.

My first boarding school was in Sussex, and I went there because it was popular with Christian Scientists. My parents, at about the time of my birth, had exchanged a rather tepid Anglicanism for the more up-and-coming doctrines of Mrs Eddy. So to St Ethelbert's I was sent. The headmaster himself was not (as the jargon of the cult used to phrase it) 'in Science'; he was, as a matter of fact, in Holy Orders. His wife, however, was, as they say, a 'keen Scientist', and every facility was given for the proper celebration of the rites. Every morning before breakfast we 'Scientists' congregated in a sort of catacomb in the basement, where the day's 'lesson' was read to us by one of the assistant-masters, Mr Learoyd, a 'keen Scientist' himself. His 'keenness' showed itself at times in other ways: he had a singularly well-developed knack of twisting arms and ears during his arithmetic classes. However, as he believed that pain was an Error of Mortal Mind, he could afford to laugh pleasantly at the tears of anguish and humiliation which his 'keenness' too often provoked. I myself was slightly prejudiced in his favour by the fact that, on the day of my arrival, he wore a spike of *Orchis morio* in his buttonhole.

But St Ethelbert's, like the war, was never quite so bad as one expected it to be. The threat of being 'sent to boarding school' had hung over me, vaguely, for years – just as the war itself was to do later on. Whenever I was more than usually ill-behaved, I was threatened with this dread banishment. After a time, since the threat was never fulfilled, 'boarding school' began to seem no more terrifying than the world of ghosts and goblins – things which one was assured didn't exist, but which one still half-believed in. Then, one day, out of the blue, came the news that I was to go to boarding school the very next term. My first reaction was a deep sense of injustice: I hadn't been particularly naughty, and the announcement had not been preluded by any of the usual threats. My mother made it suddenly one day: more in sorrow than in anger, as it were – rather as Chamberlain announced the outbreak of war in 1939.

A Munich-period of anticipation ensued – the thing was inevitable, but not yet quite real. Then trunks appeared, and lists of clothes; hairbrushes were washed, toilet-articles were labelled. When the day came, we made the journey by car; it was the first week in May, and the country was unfamiliar. I realised for the first time that there might be compensations for my exile: I should at least find some new flowers. And when we drove up the laurelled drive to the slate-roofed, red-brick building, there, sure enough, was that nice Mr Learoyd to welcome us, with the green-winged orchid in his button-hole.

*

My first new 'find' was crosswort, which was rather rare – and still is – in East Kent. *Orchis morio* grew in the school playing field. I botanised semi-secretly, with a sense of shame. Not that botany was actively discouraged: it was tolerated, but rather as religion was tolerated in the USSR. As a botanist, at St Ethelbert's, I was in a similar position to that of a priest in Soviet Russia – I could botanise, but my activities had, so to speak, no legal status, they didn't fit into the ideological framework. It would have been different if I had been 'keen' on the things that really mattered: football and cricket. But I not only intensely disliked games: I was silly enough to say so. One afternoon my fielding was such a disgrace that Mr Wilcox (another keen Scientist) degraded me from the Third Game to the Fourth, which consisted of the 'babies' of eight or nine (I was eleven). I was put in to bat. It was the one and only athletic triumph of my lifetime: I scored, I believe, about sixty-odd runs. The school was divided, for competitive purposes, into 'sets', and every day at teatime a senior boy came round the tables noting down our scores for the afternoon. On this occasion, instead of the usual 'duck' I proudly announced my enormous and unprecedented score. The note-taking senior stared, as well he might. The matter was referred to Mr Wilcox; and it was decided that, as I had been degraded to the Fourth Game, the score didn't count. After that, what little 'keenness' the system had managed to instil into me, withered in the bud. I gave up pretending. I loathed cricket with a pathological loathing, and I still do.

Scouting was another occupation in which I showed insufficient keenness. At last things came to such a pitch that Mr Wilcox, who was the scoutmaster, told me I might as well give up scouting altogether. I was a disgrace to the Troop, he said, and he never wanted to see me on parade again. Highly delighted, I put the good news into a letter home. My father, scenting some irregularity, wrote

Orchis O'Kellyii
(Glos. 24. 6. 1946.)

Orchis Morio
Green-winged Orchid.

Orchis Ustulata
[albino form]

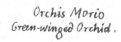

Orchis Ustulata
Dwarf Orchid
(Kent. May 1939.)

to the headmaster; and, shortly after my 'expulsion' from the Scouts, I was amazed to be taken aside by Mr Wilcox and offered a sweet. He began to talk to me in a voice of such mellifluous friendliness that I thought I must be dreaming. I seemed (he began) to have misunderstood something that he had said . . . Surely I never imagined that he had *really* said I was to leave the Scouts? Why, he hadn't even thought of such a thing, much less said it. (Another sweet.) I didn't really *still* think he'd said anything of the sort, did I?

I remained in the Scouts; I tried to be keen – but with little success. Once, when we were out on a field day, marching down a sandy lane, I saw some foxgloves growing in the hedge. Foxgloves, for me, were almost a rarity – they are not common on the chalky lands of East Kent. Without a restraining thought, I broke from the ranks and ran across to the hedge . . . The foxgloves once in my hand, I realised what I had done. But Mr Wilcox, surprisingly, remained calm and even amiable . . . Perhaps he was afraid I might write home again.

Miss Amphlett, one of the teachers, was something of a botanist; she taught the 'babies', and only the babies were supposed to be interested in flowers. I was the sole exception – a bourgeois, as it were (according to the caste system of school life) bent on declassing himself. In some respects I came to prefer the proletariat: they were not expected, for one thing, to be quite so keen.

Poor Miss Amphlett was not, after all, very reliable: she shocked me one day by identifying betony as purple loosestrife. I might have argued with her as I had argued with the lady at Folkestone about bugle and bugloss. But I had become more sophisticated (and more dishonest) by this time. If Mr Learoyd and Mr Wilcox had not taught me to be keen, they had at least taught me that it was not always wise to tell the truth.

*

At St Ethelbert's one heard a great deal about Honesty. The word was uttered in the reverent tones in which one spoke of Jesus. We were all understood to be perpetually 'on our honour' not to misbehave. There was no fixed scale of punishments: they were assumed to be unnecessary. To break the rules was dishonourable, and therefore unthinkable.

The emotional strain produced in children by such a system has to be experienced to be believed. Petty misdemeanours – failing to put one's gym shoes away in the racks provided, talking after lights-out, being late for a class – these assumed the awful complexion of mortal sins. The appalling sense of guilt thus engendered can be imagined: to talk after lights-out was equivalent to fornication, to tell a deliberate lie or to swear was only less sinful than the amusements of the Marquis de Sade.

Periodically, of course, this atmosphere of mass-guilt and persecution-mania found official outlet. On a Sunday evening after tea, it would be announced that the headmaster wanted to see us all in the Big School room. Dead silent, and consumed by an agonised apprehension, we waited, penned in our rows at the scarred, ink-stained desks. Presently the Head made his entrance: not Hitler entering the Reichstag, after the unmasking of some plot against his life, could have created a more profound effect. . . Softly the Head began to talk. 'As you know' (he would begin) 'I do not approve of using THE STICK . . .' The word fell heavily, like an expected thunderclap, upon our taut, hypnotised minds . . . 'No, I never, if I can avoid it, use The Stick. But I'm sorry to say that some of you have been found guilty of conduct which I view as DISHONOURABLE.' Another thunderclap: we wriggle in our seats . . . The soft voice continues, gradually mounting to a crescendo of horror. Somebody has broken a rule. – we are on our honour to observe the rules. If our Honour will not prevent us from breaking them – then there

remains only one alternative . . . The voice ebbs: the alternative is
not mentioned, the expected clap, the storm's peak, fails to break
over us. But we know and mutter to ourselves the unutterable: THE
STICK. And then, like a preacher turning to the East, and gabbling
'And now to God the Father, God the Son . . .' the Head's voice
suddenly drops its dramatic tones; he glances at a little list – 'I want
to see the following in my study immediately afterwards.' We listen,
with a final and increased straining of attention, to the names . . . *No,
I'm not on it* . . . The Head sweeps out, and we disperse: hysterically
laughing, jostling, catcalling in an ecstasy of relief . . . except, of
course, for those whose names were on the list. These trail slowly,
outcast and without hope of reprieve, towards The Study, where
the Head is already preparing for the sacrifice: bending, testing in
his white, rather podgy hands, the *malleus maleficarum*, the long,
lissome, willowy shape of THE STICK.

VII

ONE MORNING, halfway through that first summer term at
St Ethelbert's, a small parcel arrived for me. I undid it, and
with difficulty choked down my tears. It contained orchids found
by my old Nurse near the cottage, whither the family had already
repaired for the summer. Not for years – not till I had left school
– should I ever be able to find these orchids myself again: the
lady, the green man, the early spider – none of these orchids grew
near St Ethelbert's. For the months of May, June and July I was
condemned, for what seemed all eternity (and at that age, there
is little difference between five years and eternity) to an unhappy

exile, if not in a flowerless, at least in an orchidless world. I realised it for the first time that morning; and the yellowish spikes of the man orchid, the purple-spotted pagodas of the lady, awoke in me a nostalgia which was no ordinary homesickness, but a sense of greater loss. I realised, at last, that my childhood was nearly over.

Hurrying to be in time for Prayers (with the dread word 'Honour' echoing in my ears) I stuffed the orchids into my toothglass in the dormitory – as usual, with a sense of shame and embarrassment, rather as a priest in Soviet Russia might prepare to celebrate Mass before an assembly of keen party-members. Yet, like the priest, I was secretly assured of the validity of the rite; privately I despised my tittering companions, recognising the shallowness of their school-bred, conventional enthusiasms, knowing them incapable, in nearly every case, of even a moment's genuine emotion.

I hurried down to Prayers; but not before I had noticed, among the other orchids, an unfamiliar one: pale pink, almost white, with a crimson lip narrowly divided into four tendril-like lobes. Later in the day I unpacked Edward Step from my playbox, and once again turned up the passage about *Orchis militaris*. Had I found it at last – the military orchid? Again the annihilating, impotent nostalgia swept over me: the orchid had been found quite near our cottage, in the park in which I, myself, had found the green man, the bee, the pyramidal, for many a summer. And now, in the very first year of my absence, this distinguished stranger had elected to turn up there. Was it the military? Once again, as when Mr Bundock had brought me the lady, the old conflict was revived: I wanted my plant to be the military orchid, and knew that, by accepting Colonel Mackenzie as my authority, I was justified in so calling it. But alas! there was that qualifying clause in Edward Step about 'a subspecies known as the monkey orchid . . . with narrower divisions of the crimson lip . . . occurring in the same counties as the type, with the addition of Kent.' I looked at the plant again: the divisions of the lip could not well have been narrower; moreover, they were indubitably crimson. And the plant had been found in Kent. Reluctantly I decided that it was, after all, the 'subspecies known as the monkey orchid'. (Perhaps St Ethelbert's had already purged me of that mental dishonesty which had enabled me, years before, to label Mr Bundock's orchid the military.)

So the military orchid was, after all, still unfound. It was nice to have the monkey; but there seemed to me something slightly inferior about a 'subspecies'. The very phrases of Edward Step sounded faintly derogatory – 'a subspecies *known* as the monkey orchid' . . . it suggested the subtly insulting phraseology of the police-court: 'a woman *described* as an actress'. I could not know that my old Nurse's 'find' was to prove one of the more important plant records of the century.

A year or two later, the season was early, and the summer term must have started late; walking across the Park, on the last day of the Easter holidays, I found a single plant of the monkey orchid. By that time, I had a better idea of its importance: I had discovered that it was promoted, nowadays, to specific status, and could be ranked with the military orchid on equal terms. Later, I heard that one or two other people had found it in the same place at about this period: a lady staying in our village had drawn it, and the drawing was hung – and still hangs – in the Canterbury Museum. But after 1923 – when I found it myself – it seems to have disappeared entirely from the district. It was not till many years later that I realised how portentous its appearance there had been. Colonel Godfrey, I found, in his immense and erudite *Monograph* on the British orchids, could quote only one record for the monkey orchid in Kent – it had, apparently, been found, in the early nineteenth-century, by the Rev S.L. Jacobs, near Dover, and never rediscovered since. Colonel Godfrey, indeed was sceptical even of this single appearance, attributing it to an error of identification, or to a windblown seed.

I wrote to him, enclosing a floret of a pressed specimen, which had fortunately survived the years. He agreed that it was undoubtedly the monkey orchid. And so, in the warm, rainy days of Munich I wrote the story of the Kentish monkey for the *Journal of Botany*: remembering that morning at St Ethelbert's – the tittering boys, the sneers of Mr Wilcox, the hustle to be ready in time for Prayers; and the delicate, aristocratic flower, one of the rarest and most beautiful in the British flora, stuffed hurriedly and ignominiously into a toothglass.

The other day, I made the pilgrimage to Oxfordshire to visit the monkey orchid in its sole remaining locality: a chalky hillside overlooking the river, within too-easy reach of a popular boating resort. There it was: half-hidden among the rough grasses, smaller than its Kentish fellows, but the same charming and exquisitely formed flower that I had stuffed into my toothglass at St Ethelbert's some twenty-five years before. The botanist who accompanied me pointed out that I was possibly the only living person who had seen the monkey orchid growing in two separate British localities. If so, it is perhaps a small claim to fame: but one of which I am extremely proud.

Round about us stretched the gentle hillsides of the Thames Valley, hung with woods which, long years ago, had harboured the true military orchid. Perhaps one day it will again be found there; there seems little reason why it should have so totally vanished. Why, in any case, should the lady survive in Kent – abundantly, in some districts? And why does the monkey orchid linger in Oxfordshire?

A botanist of my acquaintance recently told me of an experience of his which occurred some years ago. He had heard that a single plant of the military still grew, carefully protected, on a private estate. He made a special journey in order to photograph it; when he arrived, however, he found that the flowers had begun to wither, and he postponed his photographing till the following year. He duly revisited the place: but the single plant – perhaps the last military orchid to survive in this country – had vanished, and has never since reappeared.

> Behind the drum and fife
> Past hawthorn-wood and hollow
> Through earth and out of life
> The soldiers follow . . .

And *Orchis militaris* has presumably gone with them – gone with scarlet and pipe-clay, with Ouida's guardsmen and Housman's lancers; gone with the concept of soldiering as a chivalric and honourable calling.

VIII

M R LEAROYD, that 'keen scientist', would sometimes give little extempore talks in the basement room at St Ethelbert's. On one such occasion, I remember, he was poking fun at some of the more flagrant errors of Mortal Mind. How silly it was, he remarked, that if one got one's feet wet, one should get a cold in one's head. That, he said, was typical of Mortal Mind. I tittered, obsequiously, with the other little 'Scientists'; but even then I realised, I think, that Mr Learoyd's play on words was typical, not so much of Mortal

Mind, as of Mrs Eddy's peculiar and paranoid theology.

But though I might sometimes be faintly critical, I was a pious enough adherent of the cult. At home, I had been a 'Scientist' merely out of deference to my family, and because they expected me to be one. At St Ethelbert's I embraced the Faith as one who was starving in the wilderness. The familiar, incantatory passages from *Science and Health* were (like the parcel of orchids) a breath of home; I had heard them from the lips of my family, and now, in the mouth of Mr Learoyd, they assumed a fresh and poignant significance.

Threatened by an attack of flu or measles, or terrified by my inability to work out an algebraic equation (in which Honour was, of course, once again involved), I would make strenuous efforts to give myself Treatment, or, as we used to say, to Know the Truth. I invented for myself a series of Christian Science Theorems, which I visualized as neatly set out in the manner of Euclid:

> God is All (this was an axiom)
> ∴ All is God
> If All is God, I must be part of God.
> But God is Good (another axiom);
>
> Therefore I must be Good – i.e., I cannot be ill
> (or be bad at maths.)
>
> QED

The fact that my temperature rose yet higher, or that the equation worked out wrong (as the case might be) didn't seriously discourage me; it was merely, I supposed, that my 'theorems' – like the equations themselves – hadn't worked out correctly. In any case, it was all very comforting; though alas! when the holidays came, there was, I regret to say, a noticeable falling-off in my pious practices.

Mortal Mind might be prolific of illusions such as Mr Wilcox and endless afternoons of cricket. But the holidays did arrive eventually, and I found myself once again at the cottage. Everything at home, I told myself firmly, was as it had been. Yet I was aware of subtle, indefinable changes. . . . I might refuse to admit them, and I was certainly unable to analyse my sensations; but the awareness set up a state of irritation and depression, I felt unsettled, possessed by a vague, irrational anxiety. Such visible, tangible changes as did occur produced in me a disproportionate unhappiness: a new wallpaper in my bedroom, some minor rearrangement in the garden. Since going to school, I clung with a ferocious conservatism to the Past: it had already become a *vert paradis*, a Land of Lost Content.

Arriving home for that first summer holiday, I visited the Igglesden children. They told me that they had found a strange plant, an orchid they thought, up in the Park. They had dug it up and planted it in their garden. I went out to investigate. The plant was withered, but recognisable – an orchid indeed, two feet high, with an inordinately long flower-spike. I looked again. Yes, there was no doubt of it. The Igglesdens had found the lizard orchid.

Once again a surge of bitterness swept over me: if only I could have found the lizard! But untold ages of school – an eternity of cricket, of Mr Wilcox, of equations – lay between me and the time when I should be able, myself, to walk across the Park in June and July. The monkey, the lizard – both had chosen this year of all years to make their portentous appearance; and I was not there to see them. Why should the Igglesdens be thus privileged, when I was not? *They* went to the village school; *they* were not exiled for nine months of the year at St Ethelbert's; and as if this were not enough, they must needs find the lizard orchid, which assuredly they didn't fully appreciate. The whole system seemed to me grossly unfair.

I consoled myself by making fireworks. At the local chemist's I obtained little packets of saltpetre, charcoal, sulphur, strontium nitrate, potassium chlorate. My mother lived in hourly terror of my blowing myself and the entire family to smithereens. Once or twice I nearly did; and a year or two later, quite unwittingly, I nearly blew up Professor Joad.

I was at Bedales by that time, and had become friendly with Julian Trevelyan, to whom, in the holidays, I sent a parcel of my home-made fireworks. Mr Joad, who was staying with the Trevelyans, was detailed, it seems, to ignite one of my maroons. Either Mr Joad was too slow, or the fuse was too short: the maroon, at any rate, exploded with an annihilating report within a few inches of the eminent philosopher's nose. Had the distance been only slightly less, the BBC might have been a different (and doubtless inferior) institution.

PART TWO

Du Côté de Chez Prufrock

I should have been a pair of ragged claws
Scuttling across the floors of silent seas.

T. S. ELIOT

I

THE ROARING TWENTIES . . ! But the label, perhaps, is a mistake. The true voice of the epoch was, surely, not a full-throated roar but a kind of exacerbated yelping; a false-virile voice tending, in moments of stress, to rise to an equivocal falsetto – half-revealing (like the voice of M. de Charlus) behind its ill-assumed masculinity a whole bevy of *jeunes filles en fleurs*. The authentic note in literature is sounded by Aldous Huxley's Mr Mercaptan – whose laughter was said, in the novel *Antic Hay,* to resemble an 'orchestra of bulls and canaries'. In fact, Mr Mercaptan, with his eighteenth-century bric-a-brac, his editions of Crébillon and Proust – Mr Mercaptan, if anybody, may be said to epitomise the period. His ineffable flat in Sloane Street surely deserves a plaque: and while they are about it, perhaps the borough council will bestow a similar honour upon that other house, nearby, where 'under the name of Monna Vanna, Mrs Shamefoot kept a shop' in Ronald Fairbank's *Vainglory.*

The War, the Boom, the Slump – events did conspire to isolate those years with a curious completeness: justifying, for once, perhaps, the slick reckoning of the gossip-writer, too ready, for the most part, thus to pigeonhole a period neatly between two noughts. The world of the Twenties existed in a kind of historical parenthesis: a timeless St Martin's Summer, in which the past was forgotten, and the future, as far as possible, ignored. No wonder that those of us who grew up during that extraordinary decade are apt to suffer from an incurable nostalgia. The typical Man of the Twenties – Prufrock or Theodore Gumbril – was but poorly adapted for the earnest, drab salvationism that came in with the Thirties; he might learn to call himself a Communist or even an Anglo-Catholic, but he remained, at bottom, an impenitent Futilitarian, whose only ethical slogan (if any) was Intellectual Honesty.

By the time I left school in 1927, the epoch had, alas! already passed its peak: legends were forming, even then, of the Heroic Age, the 'post-war' years of Dada and the *Boeuf sur le Toit*. By the end of the decade even the music halls had 'gone nostalgic' with highly successful revivals of Edwardian or wartime tunes: *A Bicycle made for Two, If you were the Only Girl in the World*. Lawrence died; Prufrock was already a High Anglican; Mr Mercaptan was well on the way to becoming a Hollywood Yogi or a Constructive Pacifist.

In 1930 appeared the first edition of Auden's *Poems*. It was the death knell of the decade, a call to order. Next year came the National Government, and with it the New Seriousness. A steady stream of expatriates began to flow homeward (second-class) from their artificial paradises in the South. Nepenthe and Trou-sur-Mer were abandoned. A cry went up from the Dôme and the Rotonde, and was echoed from a hundred delicious night-boxes. (Even the rue de Lappe felt the pinch.) Weeping, weeping multitudes drooped in the Fitzroy (lately refurbished, incongruously, with chromium stools from the wreckage of the Blue Lantern.) The intellectual chichi which had marked the vanishing era was sternly rebuked; and the strident war-cries of homocommunism echoed from Russell Square all the way to Keats Grove. A number of ageing Peter Pansies wisely fled to the country, there to cultivate their Olde Worlde gardens among the pylons and the petrol pumps; and an epoch which had begun with a bang came to an end, all too appropriately, with a whimper.

*

For myself, the period did indeed start with a bang, which, besides almost liquidating Professor Joad, shook me into an uneasy awareness of other worlds outside the green paradise which I was soon to leave. But the Whimpering Thirties were a long way ahead: in 1920 I was still at St Ethelbert's, and was to remain there for two more years. Towards the end of that time my life was overshadowed by the prospect of yet a further remove from my *paradis perdu*: in the autumn I was to go to a public school.

And to a public school I duly went; King's School, Canterbury, was my father's choice. I stayed there a week before I ran away; I was sent back, and at the end of another week, ran away again. Thus my public school career lasted a fortnight, which may, for all I know, constitute a record. No doubt I was more-than-usually sensitive, and less-than-normally plucky; but a friend of mine, who had accompanied me (with a scholarship) from St Ethelbert's and who, on both occasions, ran away with me from King's School, was to all appearance perfectly normal. He even, I seem to remember, enjoyed cricket. Unlike me, he was sent back to the school after our second escape; and as he – as well as most of our contemporaries, apparently – survived the normal four years there without going mad, I can only conclude that the system was not much more ferocious than in most places of the kind. But for me, at least, that fortnight was the final stage in a long process of prophylaxis, of immunisation against the age in which we are still living. The worst I had to fear from the war was that it would be as bad as going back to King's School again: but it never was.

Far too much has been written already about public schools, and I have no intention of adding to the literature of the subject. My experiences, I suppose, were quite usual: the ferocious initiation ceremonies, the petty cruelties and indecencies, the perpetual sense of injustice and irrational guilt. I had never thought that I should live to look back, with nostalgia, upon St Ethelbert's; yet even St Ethelbert's seemed a heaven-on-earth compared with King's School.[1] I was taken away and, with a belated wisdom, sent to Bedales; but my fortnight at a public school, if it immunised me successfully against any possible horrors which the future might hold in store, bred in me also an intolerance of tradition, a hatred of all authority and a deep-seated distrust of all institutions from which I am only now slowly beginning to recover.

Reading the innumerable accounts of the experiences by refugees who have escaped, either before or during the war, from a totalitarian to a democratic country, I have felt, over and over again, a sense of familiarity with the emotions they describe. For this was precisely my own experience when I left King's School and went to Bedales. Here, from the very first day, I was made to feel happy, and as much 'at home' as it is possible to feel at any boarding school. Nearly everybody was pleasant to me: not merely because I was a special case, but from habit, as I learnt when other new boys (and girls) arrived in subsequent terms. The perpetual cloud of fear and suspicion – which I had known at St Ethelbert's as well as at Canterbury – was suddenly, miraculously, lifted. I had not thought it possible to be 'happy' at school: but at Bedales I learnt, to my astonishment, that it was not only possible but easy.

I could make many criticisms of Bedales; co-education, as it was practised there, is possibly, I think, a mistake: for, like all small unorthodox communities which attempt to live within the framework of the status quo, a school has to make too many concessions to the principles of the outside world. Such concessions are bound to react upon and modify to some extent the principles

1. I am told that, since those days, the school has been reformed.

Cypripedium

Calceolus

Lady's Slipper

S.B.

(Norway. latitude 69° 30′N. elevation 400 ft.)

— slightly enlarged —

of the small group: and so it was at Bedales. Plainly, sexual activity couldn't be encouraged; equally plainly, in a close community of adolescents of both sexes, the sexual element must be dealt with somehow. At Bedales, the problem was solved, not exactly by ignoring sex, but by minimising its importance. To be attracted to a girl or boy and to show it was considered *silly*. In cases where 'affairs' seemed likely to have serious developments (and there were surprisingly few of these), the two parties concerned were treated to serious and sympathetic lectures in which it was pointed out that 'all that' was mere silliness; that the aim of co-education was to promote a 'healthy, natural comradeship' between the sexes, and that any deviation from this 'healthy' attitude was a kind of disloyalty to the headmaster. How such 'comradeship' between a young man and a normal adolescent girl could be 'healthy' yet entirely sexless, was not explained. Nor did one gather why 'all that' presumably ceased to be 'silly' when (at the age of eighteen or nineteen) one left school.

I think the usual accusation levelled against co-education – that it makes girls into tomboys and boys into pansies – has little justification. The effect is more insidious. Most of the girls at Bedales were perfectly feminine; the boys, far from being effeminate, tended as often as not to assume a rather over-emphatic clodhopper kind of virility – probably as a protest against so much feminine influence. What *did* happen was that the perpetual minimising of the sexual problem created a sort of emotional vacuum in the mind of the average Bedalian. I have compared Bedales to a liberal democratic state; but this anti-sexual atmosphere, created as it was by a combination of fear and self-hypnotism, had something rather fascist about it. The German in Nazi Germany, who was repeatedly told that the Jews were subhuman criminals, may have begun by doubting the assertion; subsequently he found it convenient to pay lip service to official opinion; in his own mind, he would learn to avoid the subject of the Jews: better not to think than to harbour 'dangerous thoughts'. Finally, in most cases, his own former opinions were replaced by the official attitude.

I don't suggest, of course, that sex at Bedales was regarded as the Jews were in Germany. But, if Hitler had taken it into his head to convince the German people that sex was 'silly', it is conceivable that he might have succeeded: there is something in common, after all, between the chronic idealism of the average German (especially when canalised completely by the State) and the state of mind of an English adolescent in a large boarding school.

But if the atmosphere at Bedales was anti-sexual, if inconvenient facts were gingerly skated over, the school was, I think, in other respects, a successful experiment. Spartan as it was, the spartan element was combined with humanity and kindness. Bullying was very rare; athleticism was encouraged, but not exalted above other activities. One was, indeed, adjured to be 'keen', just as at St Ethelbert's; but I soon found, to my astonishment, that one was allowed to be keen on other things besides cricket – for instance, botany. As to the school work itself, there were, admittedly, serious weaknesses in the system: it was too easy – at least during one's last year or two at school – to avoid doing more work than one wanted to. The curriculum itself was a hybrid product, which had grown out of a series of experiments: the Dalton System, the 'Laboratory' plan, Montessori, and what not. When I first went to Bedales, the 'Individual' system was in operation: for so many hours a day one was free to work at whatever one liked – Geography, Drawing, Latin, Mathematics. A teacher was posted in the appropriate classroom to oversee and encourage such 'individualists' as chose to turn up. Naturally, some forms of 'individual activity' were more popular than others: the carpentry shop, the book-binding room, the studio were usually crowded out. I remember that my first two or three days at school were spent almost entirely in the Studio. Later on, the system was tightened up, and by the time I left, was not very different from that of an ordinary school. Even so, it was possible to slack almost to one's heart's content. Once I had passed the School Certificate and Responsions, nobody cared a hoot what I did – with the result that, when I got to Oxford, I was totally unable to construe a simple bit of Latin prose, and consequently distinguished myself by failing in the Law Prelim, at the end of my first year.

II

M R BICKERSTETH, the biology master, was rather a misfit, I fancy, at Bedales; he was terrifically 'keen' – so much so, that I was uneasily reminded of Mr Wilcox and Mr Learoyd at St Ethelbert's. Fortunately for me, however, most of his keenness was centred upon botany, and in particular upon orchids. Every summer a 'Show' was arranged in the Biology lab – rows of labelled plant specimens in jam pots. The 'Show' soon became my particular province. I began slowly to realise that botany, which for me had been up till now a semi-secret and rather shameful hobby, was in fact a recognised science; and I was appalled by my ignorance. I set about, energetically, to repair some of my worst omissions; Edward Step was discarded (reluctantly) for Bentham and Hooker or Hayward's *Botanist's Pocket-Book* (edited by the redoubtable Dr Druce), and I was surprised at the number of plants I had never heard of.

Nonetheless, I was able to impress Mr Bickersteth by some of my Kentish 'finds', and the lady orchid, the spider and the green man were duly exhibited in the show. Parcels of plants, too, would arrive from other parts of the country, and even from abroad, for Mr Bickersteth's enthusiasm was not confined to the local flora. One morning a parcel arrived from, I think, Switzerland. Mr Bickersteth opened it in considerable excitement: I think he knew what was inside. He peered beneath the enveloping moss, and a hoot of joy escaped him as his suspicion was confirmed. Tenderly, he lifted the plant from its packing, and held it out for my inspection.

It was the military orchid.

True, it was a foreign specimen, and I had not found it myself; but there it was, *Orchis militaris* beyond a doubt: not Edward Step, not even Colonel Mackenzie could have called it anything else. It was not unlike the monkey orchid, but with a longer, more cylindrical spike, and broader divisions of the lip. There was nothing very military about it after all: the name presumably refers to the helmet-shaped 'hood' of the flower, or possibly to the faintly anthropoid, reddish lip, but the resemblance to a soldier was hard to detect.

More realistic in its mimicry was the lizard orchid, which my old Nurse discovered, that same season, in the locality where the Igglesdens had found it a year or so previously. Mr Bickersteth's enthusiasm, when the parcel arrived, was noisy and prolonged. To exhibit the lizard orchid *and* the military orchid in his show, in a single season, exceeded the scope even of his wide-flung ambition. Not content, however, with these two prizes, he had obtained, before the end of the term, specimens of the red helleborine and the lady's slipper, as well as *Orchis laxiflora,* the Jersey orchid, from the Channel Islands.

To myself, the assembled orchids, in their jam pots and potted-meat jars, were so many symbols of a happiness which was so acute, so consciously enjoyed, that it filled me with a kind of superstitious fear. To be so happy at school seemed to me against nature; I could only marvel, as the exciting, sunlit weeks slipped by, that I had actually forgotten to look forward to the holidays. Of course, it would be nice when they came . . . but my half-hearted anticipation was largely a matter of habit and schoolboy convention. I had never been so happy or felt so well in my life before: not, at any rate, since I first went to school. My school life, up till now, had passed in an uninterrupted longing for the holidays: and in the holidays, my happiness – itself based mainly on the fact of not being at school, rather than on any more positive emotion – had been invariably tainted with the prospect of the coming term.

I had become, in fact, a different person. Even my physical and social timidity had largely been cured by the tolerant, easy-going atmosphere of Bedales. I learnt to swim; and I began to make friends. My stupidity at Arithmetic, instead of being regarded as a breach of Honour, or an insult to the master concerned, was treated with helpful kindliness. Even cricket and football came to seem merely boring instead of a source of terror. I had gone to Bedales in the Christmas term, after leaving Canterbury; by the following summer, I had become transformed from a 'difficult', neurotically timid and generally unsatisfactory child, into something approaching a healthy, normal schoolboy.

On Saturday and Sunday afternoons we would set off on our bicycles – Mr Bickersteth, myself, and one or two other enthusiasts – for Harting or Selborne, or over the downs towards Winchester, in search of some unfound rarity. And after the long, torrid hours spent wading through marshes, or climbing over chalk downs, we would arrive back, sweating, our vascula crammed with specimens. Perhaps we had found the frog orchid on War Down, or the violet helleborine on Selborne Hanger; or I had seen sundew or bog asphodel for the first time in Woolmer Forest. It was seldom that the vasculum didn't contain something which made the journey worthwhile and exciting. Arriving back at the school, we would bathe, then eat an enormous tea; and happiness would blossom in my mind like some brilliant, alien flower which has established itself in homely surroundings, where its splendour is still a source of surprise, almost of suspicion. It was as though one should suddenly come upon the military orchid on a waste patch in some dingy suburb, among mugwort and goosefoot and all the squalid weeds bred by indifference and neglect.

After tea, I would return to the lab, to put our specimens in water, and to gloat, once again, on the fabulous lineaments of the military and the lizard. And later (if it was a Sunday) there was 'Jaw'.

This was the disrespectful name bestowed, by staff and children alike, on the Sunday evening service, at which, in rotation, some member of the staff gave an address. The service was held in a building imitated, I think, from some mediaeval tithe barn or Hall of Justice: arched beams of unvarnished oak supported the roof, and through the narrow, latticed windows, the evening sun fell softly upon the piano, the school orchestra and the assembled school. The service was strictly undenominational: the music ranged from plainchant or the Agincourt Song to the brighter, more uplifting melodies of Hymns Ancient and Modern. The words were as varied as the tunes; and the prayers had a tentative, rather apologetic air – God, one inferred, was addressed rather hypothetically: at mention of His name, the speaker would usually pause, ever so slightly, as though adding, silently, the cautious qualification: 'If You exist'.

After the service, the entire school filed past the assembled staff, shaking hands: a ritual in which the staff – like officers in the matter of saluting – had the worst of it. At the end of the row stood the headmaster, J.H. Badley – the pioneer of co-education in England: tall, broad-shouldered, with grizzled hair and beard, his eyes kindly but grave behind his spectacles; attired invariably in a grey flannel suit, gym shoes and a scarlet tie.

And coming out of the hall, the school buildings, the tall, high-windowed rooms, the echoing, glass-roofed quadrangle – all the quotidian background of the school life – seemed transfigured, fringed with a romantic haze of happiness, a happiness tainted, already, for me, with a foreknowledge that it could not be lasting. For my sense of the past was too strong to allow me to surrender, for long, to such a calm and sunlit contentment. Try as I might to forget, memories of Canterbury or St Ethelbert's would recur; I would remember, too, that once I had been happy before; and images of Sandgate, of Gaudeamus, of our country cottage would merge with the symbols of my present happiness, infecting them with melancholy; and my eyes would prick with tears, as I realised suddenly that this summer evening, too, would pass at length into the hoarded repository of my memories, irretrievable, never to be repeated: a picture to be placed alongside other pictures – evenings at the cottage, Mr Bundock bringing home the lady orchid, my moonlight romance with Miss Trumpett, or our home at Sandgate, with the sound of the sea stealing, like a muted plainchant, through windows opening upon the summer garden.

Such moments seemed to demand some form of outward expression, and I decided to embark upon a love affair. It began almost by accident: I was sitting in the library, where one was not allowed to talk; a girl was sitting at the same table, and for some innocent

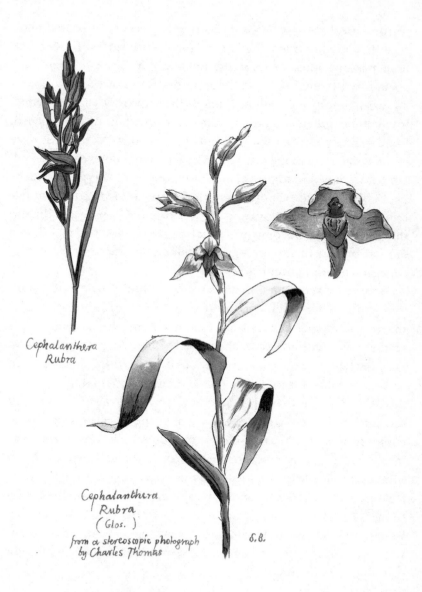

*Cephalanthera
Rubra*

*Cephalanthera
Rubra
(Glos.)*
*from a stereoscopic photograph
by Charles Thomas*

S.B.

reason – probably I wanted to borrow her pencil – I passed her a note. Later, when I left the library, there were titters: Brooke had been passing notes to Dorothy. Evidently it was an 'affair': the dormitory that night could talk of nothing else.

I was painfully embarrassed, but at the same time rather excited. It would be rather fun, I thought, to have an affair. As it happened, I had scarcely noticed the girl; but the next day I contrived, once more, to sit at the same table during prep. More notes were passed. Dorothy seemed to approve, in a rather negative way; at least, she didn't object. That evening, after prayers, we stood together for five minutes under an archway in the quadrangle, saying goodnight: this was the prescribed nightly ritual for those who 'had a girl', and our liaison was thereby recognised, put on an official basis, like an engagement announcement in *The Times*.

Dorothy (a very suitable name) was a plump, pasty-faced girl, two years older than myself; besides being quite unattractive, she was monumentally boring. I cannot remember a single word of the conversations we exchanged: I preferred passing notes in the library, anyway, since this required less effort, and appeared agreeably conspiratorial. The whole thing soon bored me to tears: the excitement of 'having a girl' began to pall, and I sensed that the elder boys and girls – and probably the staff as well – were deprecating my 'silliness'. Silliness it undoubtedly was in my case: there was about as much sex involved as there had been in my 'romance' with Miss Trumpett at the age of six. What Dorothy's feelings were I cannot imagine: at any rate, she was soon unfaithful to me. One night, coming out rather late from prayers, I found her standing under the archway with a new companion. I passed her without even saying goodnight, and went up to bed with a sense of profound and unmitigated relief.

III

> So, some tempestuous morn in early June,
> When the year's primal burst of bloom is o'er,
> Before the roses and the longest day –
> When garden walks and all the grassy floor
> With blossoms red and white of fallen May
> And chestnut flowers are strewn. . . .

IT WOULD BE POSSIBLE, I fancy, to compile a small anthology of English verse reflecting this same elegiac mood of frost-in-May and the ruins of an English Spring. It was a genre which, when I first started reading poetry, I found particularly sympathetic; hearing J.H. Badley read aloud Arnold's lines, on just such a stormy summer morning, I felt that this was the kind of poetry I really liked: an evocation of country scenes accompanied by a sense of melancholy and regret.

> So have I heard the cuckoo's parting cry,
> From the wet field, through the vext garden trees,
> Come with the volleying rain and tossing breeze:
> *The bloom is gone, and with the bloom go I!*

Later, too, there was Housman, in similar strain:

> The chestnut casts his flambeaux, and the flowers
> Stream from the hawthorn on the wind away,
> The doors clap to, the pane is blind with showers.
> Pass me the can, lad; there's an end of May.

And that poem, too, of Wilfred Gibson, an ubiquitous anthology piece, and the text for many a rhyme sheet and poker-worked calendar, which I found very moving:

> A bird among the rain-wet lilac sings –
> But we, how shall we turn to little things
> And listen to the birds and winds and streams
> Made holy by their dreams,
> Nor feel the heartbreak in the heart of things?

I had begun, by this time, myself to write poetry; and I was acutely aware – or so I like to think – of the 'heartbreak in the heart of things'. It is a common enough symptom of puberty: an *Anthology of Bedales Verse* which I still possess is full of poems by children of twelve or thirteen about Eternity, fading flowers and unrequited love. A useful corrective, in my own case, was the discovery of T.S. Eliot, whom the English master referred to as 'Futurist'. Mr Eliot might well have demurred at being labelled as a disciple of Marinetti; but at that time – with *The Waste Land* fresh from the press – it was not generally realised that Alfred Prufrock was at heart a royalist and an Anglo-Catholic. *The Waste Land* seemed extremely modern and revolutionary.

In my readings of poetry, I was apt to be rather uncritical; but in one respect, I outdid the most academic of textual critics in my pedantry. Inaccurate references to plants were liable to provoke me into a positively Housmanly cantankerousness.

> And round green roots and yellowing stalks I see
> Pale blue convolvulus in tendrils creep. . . .

Blue? In later editions *blue* is duly corrected to *pink,* for Arnold, unlike most English poets, was generally pretty accurate in his botany.

> I know these slopes; who knows them if not I? . . .
> But many a dingle on the loved hillside,
> With thorns once studded, old, white-blossom'd trees,

> Where thick the cowslips grew, and far descried
> High tower'd the spikes of purple orchises,
> Hath since our day put by
> The coronals of that forgotten time. . . .

Given the Oxfordshire background, it was tempting to speculate if some at least of the 'orchises', whose passing the poet laments, were *Orchis simia* or *Orchis militaris*. But Arnold's references to plants – and *Thyrsis* and *The Scholar Gypsy* are full of them – are nearly always pleasingly exact. For example:

> Some country-nook, where o'er thy unknown grave
> Tall grasses and white flowering nettles wave,
> Under a dark, red-fruited yew-tree's shade. . . .

That is ecologically correct – and being so, for a botanist enhances the poem's effect. But turn from Arnold to Keats, for instance:

> I cannot see what flowers are at my feet,
> Nor what soft incense hangs upon the boughs,
> But in embalmed darkness guess each sweet . . .

And so on, finishing up with a vague reference to violets and eglantine. The lines might be quoted as typical of poet's botany. Shelley is the same, and most of the Romantics: where flowers are introduced, the poet tends to become vague, or to fall back on eglantine and roses, or, else to plump for half-mythical but resounding names like amaranth and moly. Keats does indeed mention wolfsbane as a poisonous plant, and may have meant *Aconitum napellus,* but it is highly doubtful.

Clare and Crabbe are justly famed, of course, for their flower poetry; and Crabbe, at least, was a botanist, and seldom makes a mistake:

> Around the dwellings docks and wormwood rise;
> Here the strong mallow strikes her slimy root,
> Here the dull nightshade hangs her deadly fruit:
> On hills of dust the henbane's faded green
> And pencill'd flower of sickly scent is seen. . . .

Though even here I doubt the presence, on the Suffolk coast, of the deadly nightshade: I suspect that Crabbe meant the black nightshade, or possibly bittersweet, neither of which is particularly deadly.

But if poets can claim their traditional licence, what are we to say of prose writers? Most of them are worse than the poets, and with less excuse. Even the most self-consciously rural of novelists seem incapable of being factually accurate about flowers; what makes matters worse is their pretentiousness, their air of omniscience. No novelist would write so cocksurely about numismatics, for instance, or toxicology, without checking his statements; yet anyone can write nonsense about flowers and get away with it.

An exception was D.H. Lawrence; a genuine lover of flowers, he took the trouble to be accurate about them. Another, rather surprisingly, was Proust. He seldom describes flowers for their own sake, but how many of his similes and analogies are botanical, and how exact they are! Sometimes, indeed, he becomes almost too technical, as in the parallel which he draws between the Charlus-Jupien encounter (in *Sodome et Gomorrhe)* and the fertilisation of the orchid belonging to Oriane de Guermantes. We are supposed to be a nation of flower lovers; but as far as novel writing goes, it has taken a Frenchman to tap the resources of botany.

The Elizabethans are popularly supposed to have been, as writers, particularly botanophile: but D.H. Lawrence, I think, summed the matter up when he called their imagery 'upholstered'. Their lilies and violets and gillyflowers are seldom more than conventional decoration. Shakespeare seems to have had a genuine taste for flowers, however – and wild ones at that; moreover, he is often unusually explicit – though sometimes his nomenclature has given rise to confusion, as with the

> . . . long purples,
> That liberal shepherds give a grosser name,
> But our cold maids do Dead-men's fingers call them . . .

Millais, in his picture of Ophelia, assumes that Shakespeare meant the purple loosestrife: but the loosestrife was never called dead-men's fingers, nor, for that matter, by any 'grosser name'. Dead-men's fingers, in fact, refers to one or other of the palmate-rooted orchises, and is also loosely used for *Orchis mascula,* one of the round-tubered species, all of which were given 'grosser names', not only by liberal shepherds, but by the early herbalists; the reason being that the twin tubers suggested a pair of testicles. (This seems to have accounted, too, for the ancient use of orchis roots as an aphrodisiac – presumably on the principle of sympathetic magic. 'Satyrion' is mentioned by Petronius and Pliny, and under the name of Salep was still sold in this country up till the early nineteenth century. It is still used in Turkey, and considered to have mildly stimulant properties.)

Some of the older references to flowers in literature raise the interesting problem of how much (or how little) the flora of this country has changed in the last three or four hundred years. Accurate plant records, of course, were almost unheard of before the nineteenth century; and most theories about the British flora, as it existed before that period, are the purest speculation. For example, Shakespeare mentions the oxlip, as a familiar wild flower. Now the oxlip, today, is a rare and local plant, confined to a few districts in East Anglia. Presuming that Shakespeare meant by oxlip the flower which now bears that name – and it is quite possible that he meant something else – the question arises: was the oxlip, in Shakespeare's time, a common and widely distributed plant, which has since become scarce? It is possible, of course, that Shakespeare merely used the name 'oxlip' because he liked it; but this, with Shakespeare, is unusual. Some of the plants he mentions can still be found in the localities which he specifies – a classical example is the samphire on the Dover cliffs. The supposition that the oxlip was common in his day, and has since become rare; that this can happen, is proved by plenty of modern instances – including *Orchis militaris*.

IV

B<small>UT MY MAIN OCCUPATION</small>, during those last terms at Bedales, was writing 'novels'. I wrote at least half a dozen: some of them I still possess – closely written, in thick, cloth-covered school exercise books on both sides of the paper. In 1939, at the outbreak of war, I disinterred them from my old school playbox. . . . *Il faut, Nathanaël, que tu brûles en toi tous les livres*. . . . Yes, I thought, it would have saved a lot of trouble if I had burnt them 'within myself', instead of allowing them to take this too, too solid form. *Quand aurons-nous brûlés tous les livres?* I thought, feeding the fire with yet another abortive adolescent masterpiece.

At the top of the box was my earliest 'novel': it was called (very suitably) *Clouds,* and must have been written when I was about fifteen. I turned the closely written pages – the writing was formed and legible, almost without corrections. That fatal facility, I thought – I must have possessed it even then. The novel, needless to say, was about the country; 'plot' and character, indeed, were plainly the

S.B.

Orchis
Laxiflora
The Jersey Orchid
(Guernsey 1946.)

merest pegs on which to hang my rhapsodical descriptions of spring
in the Kentish woods. A rather dim young man called Ian lived near
Canterbury: he was married, but his wife didn't like the country,
or perhaps she merely didn't like him. In any case, Ian was very
unhappy, and the 'story' consisted almost entirely of descriptions
of his long, lonely walks through the countryside, interspersed with
reflections upon God and War and the League of Nations – topics
about which, in real life, my feelings at that time were singularly
lukewarm.

But it wasn't the world of the novel itself that came back to me
as I turned the pages, squatting on the floor by the playbox: what
I chiefly remembered was sitting in the library at Bedales, the hot
air from the heating apparatus wafting a smell of dust and muddy
football boots among the high shelves, the autumnal trees dripping
outside the windows, and a pianist in the neighbouring hall repeating
over and over again the same passage from Rachmaninov's *Prelude*
in C sharp minor. The *Prelude* itself, hackneyed as it is, became
evocative years after, reminding me of just this complex of feelings
and sensations; the dusty indoor-warmth after football, the autumn
dusk falling over the school buildings, the dripping trees – and the
warm, almost sexual feeling of release as my pen raced over the lined
paper, turning out page after page of facile, middlebrow prose. It was
at least, I suppose, a more rewarding occupation than passing notes
to Dorothy.

There were several more 'novels', on similar lines, after this: then
there came a complete break. *Shepherd's Hey* (which must have
been my fifth or sixth 'novel') was prefaced by a quotation from
Aldous Huxley. I had read *Crome Yellow* and *Antic Hay,* and a
new world had opened for me.

Both in my prose and in real life I became 'a little weary', at
the same time affecting a Gumbrilesque cynicism towards all the

things which I had previously taken seriously. Up till this time I had continued to cling, rather half-heartedly, to Christian Science – or at least to a personal, rather heretical and pantheistic version of the Faith; Mrs Eddy, however, could not long survive the atmosphere of Mr Mercaptan's *dix-huitième* boudoir. *Shepherd's Hey* was nothing more or less than a Huxleyfied version of my daily life at school; my friends were portrayed without the least disguise; whole conversations went down almost verbatim. True, some of the characters – particularly myself – tended to speak the Huxley dialect: but after all, I was trying hard to speak it in real life. I wrote chapter after chapter with immense enjoyment: there seemed no reason why the book should ever come to an end.

A shameless exhibitionist, I showed the manuscript to my friends, who were all depicted in their worst lights: after all, I had been merciless enough to myself. With the fever of a convert at his first confession, I had described minutely my most intimate sexual preoccupations; what would have happened if a member of the staff had got hold of the book, I cannot imagine.

While I wrote it, I identified myself so completely with the hero that I find it almost impossible to remember, nowadays, whether certain episodes really happened, or whether I invented them. But if Maurice, the hero, was based on myself, it is no exaggeration to say that I came to be based largely on Maurice. Our development – Maurice's and mine – was a sort of race: sometimes I was ahead, sometimes Maurice. If I read Verlaine, Maurice had read him within the week; if Maurice was reading Joyce I was wrestling with *Ulysses* as soon as a copy could be obtained.

On the whole I was honest: I didn't often allow Maurice's cultural activities to eclipse my own. It was more of an effort, though, to keep up with his emotional development; in his sexual life Maurice was as unenterprising and as much frustrated as I was myself; but there came a time when he threatened to put into action what had remained, for me, the most cerebral and inoperative of desires. Reluctantly, and with a sense of rather noble renunciation, I brought the book to a sudden and somewhat unsatisfactory conclusion.

But I had reckoned without Maurice: with the best intentions on my part, he simply refused – once having been set in motion – to lie down and die. Soon I had begun another novel about him; and in this, alas! wish-fulfilment had triumphed completely. But how I enjoyed writing it! The book was, I suppose, chiefly a kind of protest – begun in the previous 'novel' – against Bedales, and the depressing fact that I was still at school. I felt grown-up, and I was chafing at the restrictions of school life, which I couldn't be bothered, now, even to satirise: I merely wanted to escape from it. Maurice was already at Oxford: and the fact that I hadn't caught up with him seemed a mere historical accident.

Nonetheless, the life of the school made certain demands upon me: I became a prefect, which gave me a certain amount of authority (though far less than at a public school) and involved a fair number of duties. Moreover, though I might have decided to be Literary, my liking for botany persisted. It became, once again, a semi-secret and rather shameful passion: unworthy, as I considered, of an aesthete and a decadent. The trips to Harting or Winchester continued, but coming back in the evening, sweating, happy and healthier than ever, I would retire to the library and write: a new chapter of Maurice's saga, or perhaps a poem – probably a villanelle – about fading flowers and spiritual corruption, and how everything was unbearably sad, and Life was Futile.

It would be highly entertaining to myself – but not, alas! to anybody else – to follow the subsequent career of the unfortunate Maurice. But the later volumes of his saga were committed, perhaps wisely, to the flames. . . . It is sufficient to say that his behaviour pattern conformed impeccably to type. Having been sent down from Oxford, he worked for a time (as might have been expected) in a publisher's office; frequented the bars and night-boxes of Bloomsbury and Montparnasse; paid visits to Trou-sur-Mer, and nearly (but not quite) became a Communist. Never altogether happy in Mr Mercaptan's boudoir, he could never, on the other hand, quite bring himself to follow in the footsteps of Alfred J. Prufrock along that *via media* which led, so consolingly (if somewhat painfully) out of the Waste Land. . . . Nor, like his creator, did he ever succeed in finding the military orchid. He died in 1939, murmuring passages from *The Hollow Men,* and regretting the *paradis perdu* of a vanished age: a good old-fashioned Futilitarian to the last.

PART THREE

The High Mountains of Clova

Now let's think what shall we throw
what
    do
       you
          think, a
bomb? No let me suggest a Commode

CLERE PARSONS

1

M AJOR WILMOTT WAS *alakefak*: so much so, that it was difficult to get him to do any work at all.

'Anybody I ought to see this morning?' he would say, coming into the clinic tent at about half-past ten. Fifty or sixty patients had been waiting outside since nine o'clock: their restive noises could be heard beyond the tent-flap – a subdued bourdon of whispering, scraps of swing, muttered curses, shuffling feet.

'You ought to see the patients in A tent,' I said.

The major looked bored.

'How many's that?'

'About fifty.'

'H'm – yes. Well . . . the fact is I'm really rather busy. I promised the surgeon I'd go over and look at a case of his. And the staff sergeant's waiting for me to go through the monthly returns. Could you sort out the most – um – urgent ones, and I'll run through them?'

'Very good, Sir.'

I sorted out the case-cards as best I could, while the major had a cup of tea with the Sister. The tea- drinking took rather a long time; another MO came in, and the major seemed to have forgotten his patients entirely. At last I went to remind him – taking the cards of those I had weeded out as 'urgent'.

'H'm – yes. You know, I really ought to get over to the Surgical Division. I promised to be there by eleven.'

No doubt, I thought, there was another cup of tea waiting for him in the Surgical Sister's bunk.

'Really, you know,' he went on, 'I don't think I need see all this lot today. They're all on treatment, are they not?'

'Oh, yes, Sir, they're all on treatment.'

The major looked at me, and his eyes twinkled.

'I always say that, in dermatology, there's a great deal to be said for leaving things to Nature. One shouldn't over-treat skin conditions; let Nature take its course. H'm – what do you think, Edwards?' He turned to the other MO, a captain.

'Oh, I agree, Sir. Nothing like letting Nature take her course.'

'Er – well, yes. I think we might leave these over till tomorrow, don't you?'

As clinic-orderly I was of course only too pleased: it meant an hour's less work, and I could go and help with the treatments.

'I think you ought to see Boughton,' I said.

'Boughton? Boughton?' The major twinkled again. 'Ah, yes: how does it go?' And suddenly he began to sing:

> How beautiful they are –
> The lordly ones
> Te *tum*-titty *tum* –
> In the hol-low hills . . .

'No, Sir,' I said, 'not Rutland Boughton – Private Boughton, that impetigo case with the high temperature.'

'Oh, yes, Boughton. Of course. Well, we'll see Boughton. Better send those other blokes away till tomorrow. *Tum*-titty *tum* – in the hollow hills.'

I sent the other blokes away. They were not unjustly rather annoyed, 'Cor, what sort of place is this?' they said. 'Don't you ever get no —ing treatment? I'm not standing for this. I'll see my

OC about this, I will.' Then we saw Boughton.

'H'm, yes. I think we'd better evacuate him. It's no good trying to treat a case of that kind up here in the blue. No facilities, no facilities. Fix it up with the Medical Wardmaster, will you?'

The major was very keen on evacuating his patients; it saved no end of trouble.

Coming out of the tent, he hummed the *Faery Song* again.

'I'm afraid the colonel takes a very poor view of me,' he remarked. 'I was trying over Brahms's Sapphic Ode at the mess piano before breakfast this morning. I feel he took a very poor view of the whole proceeding. H'm, yes. A very poor shufti indeed. . . . Oh, by the way, one more thing: I wonder if you'd mind running down to the Royal Engineers' mess with a message for the Colonel? I'll give you a chitty – you needn't wait for a reply.' I had a cup of tea while he wrote out the chitty. Then I walked down to the RE mess.

We were stationed near a small Italian colonial town, in the Cyrenaican greenbelt. The hospital, formerly an Italian military one, lay on a slight hill: all around, the vast open countryside stretched away for miles; highly cultivated, yet strangely desolate, a land half-reclaimed from the desert. To the north, a range of low, rocky hills broke up the landscape; but to southwards, the cornfields – already burnt golden by the hot March sun – seemed to roll away endlessly towards the heart of Africa. Disposed in regular patterns across their vast expanse, the square white farmhouses of the Italian colonists looked like toys.

The hospital itself was built round an enormous quadrangle of bare sand. The white, arcaded buildings had a certain Italianate grace, and the whole disposition of them suggested, nostalgically, some piazza in southern Italy. In a British colony, I thought, the hospital would have been of redbrick and corrugated iron, and the whole place would have looked exactly like Aldershot.

Over the sandy quadrangle tiny sky-blue irises grew in profusion, springing nakedly from the dry, trodden soil. Walking across, I tried to translate the fascist slogans which were painted on the walls of the buildings:

MEGLIO UN GIORNO DA LEONE CHE CENTO ANNI DA PECORA.

I knew that one, of course. Then there was the one about machine guns (wasn't it Marinetti's?) – something about the song of the *mitragliatrice* being the Song of Life. And on every other wall, in enormous blue letters:

CREDERE, OBBEDIRE, COMBATTERE.

We were a VD Treatment Unit, attached to a General Hospital; but Major Wilmott had been prevailed upon to 'lend' half a dozen of his orderlies to the Skin Division, and to offer his own services in his capacity of Dermatologist. We were accommodated in two tents, with a Sister of the Queen Alexandra's to supervise. In practice, the Sister's nursing duties were confined to making tea; I dealt with the case-cards and the running of the clinic, and helped with the treatments. It was a cushy job, and I enjoyed it.

Walking down to the RE mess, I passed our own quarters: rows of billets which looked like a cross between stables and pigsties. They had been used formerly by Italian colonial troops, and were full of bugs. But between the two rows of billets was an avenue of mulberries and acacias, and the place looked clean and charming in the spring sunshine. Outside the treatment rooms, the VD patients squatted in the sun, waiting for their irrigations or injections; they looked browned-off. One of them, a Libyan Arab, was playing some kind of reed instrument, which sounded oddly like bagpipes. Along the paths and on the banks, grew a profusion of the starry clover – *Trifolium stellatum*, one of the rarest plants in the British flora, confined, in Britain, to a patch of foreshore at Shoreham, in Sussex. It was pleasant, but rather shocking, to see it growing so abundantly in the middle of a VD hospital in Libya.

My friend Kurt Schlegel, an Austrian Jew enlisted in the British Army in Palestine, emerged from one of the treatment rooms as I passed. He seemed excited.

'What balls-up then is this?' he exclaimed, without preliminary, in his fluent but very peculiar English. 'I write up all the twelve-forty-sevens for that bastard, give them to him, and he then say: No, Schlegel, I do not want that you write up my cards. I do them myself. So then, you bastard, I say, you —ing do them yourself.'

'I bet you didn't call him a bastard,' I said.

'No, in effect I did not. But for why should I his bloody cards write, and then like a child be treated?'

'Never mind. We're both on half-day today. Coming out for a walk?'

Kurt looked black.

'It is very well for you,' he muttered. 'You work on Skins. Very nice, very cushy.'

'I like Johnny Wilmott.'

'Yes, I think he is the true English gentleman, isn't it?'

'Except that he's Scotch.'

'He cares also a — for his orderlies.'

'I expect that's because he's a gentleman.' Kurt nodded.

'It is to expect,' he agreed. 'Where then do you now go?'

I told him where I now went, and left him.

The RE mess, when I arrived, seemed deserted. I went into the hallway: the place had been a small country villa, the property perhaps of some richer colonist. There were polished tables and chairs in the hall, and the whole place looked oddly unmilitary. On

one of the tables stood a bowl full of tall, pinkish flowers. I went
to look at them: I looked again; at last I took one out of the bowl.
Yes, there could be no doubt: the plant I held in my hand was the
military orchid.

At that moment a woman emerged from the kitchen-quarters.
Johnny Wilmott had warned me about her: she was Italian, but
spoke a little French. I gave her the major's note; then I asked her
about the orchid: did she know where it grew? She didn't. Who had
found it? *M. le Colonel* had found it, she said. Was *M. le Colonel* in
the mess, I enquired? At that moment I, a private, would have been
quite prepared to beard the colonel in his bedroom, or even in the
lavatory, had he been there. But he was not. *Mi dispiace*, said the
woman, *c'est dommage*. . . . But the colonel wasn't there, and she
had no idea where he had found the plant. *Nella campagna, dans
la campagne*, no doubt. I asked if I might take a specimen. *Mais
volontiers*, she replied.

I left her, and, bearing a fine specimen of the military orchid,
walked back toward the hospital. I left the orchid in my billet,
and returned to the Skin tent. When the major returned, I told
him about my discovery. He was sympathetic, and promised to
ask the colonel of the RE unit where he had found it. I waited a
few days, and then broached the subject again. The major was
vague: he hadn't had an opportunity. . . . The days passed, weeks
passed. I lacked the courage to return to the RE mess myself;
and Johnny Wilmott no doubt felt that to approach a colonel
whom he scarcely knew, merely to oblige one of his orderlies who
happened to be a botanist, was hardly befitting to a Major *and* a
Specialist-Dermatologist.

*

Owing, therefore, to the exigencies of military etiquette, the military orchid had eluded me once again. I consoled myself, however, on a closer examination of the plant, by deciding that it was not, after all, the true military. The divisions of the mid-lobe were too narrow: it was probably an 'intermediate' between *Orchis militaris* and *Orchis simia*. (When I returned to England the plant was identified as a variety *tridentata* of *Orchis militaris*.)

And shortly afterwards the Unit moved to Tripoli.

The military orchid might have eluded me once again. But Cyrenaica had its compensations. The north African flora is not unlike that of southern Europe; and very much more 'European', of course, than that of South Africa. Botanising round Cape Town, on the way out, I found the flora entirely bewildering: it was difficult to assign a particular plant to any family, much less to a species. But in Cyrenaica, the flowers were at least half-familiar; one could usually spot at a glance which family they belonged to. And in many cases they were plants which, in England, are exceedingly rare. Such as, for example, the wild gladiolus, which in March grew in great drifts in the cornfields; or the starry clover, the commonest weed of the wayside banks. In the cornfields, too, there were the two *Adonises* – the scarlet one, an English rarity, and the yellow species, unknown in Britain. And everywhere grew the big, yellow ranunculus, as large as a poppy, which, earlier in the year, had covered the desert round Tobruk. And in midwinter, the meadows near the hospital had been starred with a small lily, bluish-purple and cold as Sirius, flickering like a weak spirit-flame among the drenched grasses.

After Alamein, the chase across the desert, the fall of Tripoli, the landings in Algeria, it began to seem that the war might soon be over: the 'end of term' was in sight, I would be going home for holidays.

In Tripoli we had six weeks in transit, with nothing to do; if one could avoid the vigilance of the staff sergeant after breakfast, one could hitchhike down to the beach and bathe. I spent a weekend, unofficially, with a friend of mine, a masseur at a Convalescent Depôt along the coast, on the way to Homs. He was a musician and a Catholic convert; in the afternoon he played the Ravel *Sonatine* on the piano in the Garrison Theatre, and in the evening, sitting on the sand beneath the tamarisks on the edge of the desert, he chanted the *Veni Sancte Spiritus* from the Sarum Gradual.

All this was, naturally, too good to last; the General Hospital to which we were attached 'borrowed' us for ward-duties. Casualties were streaming in from the Sicily landings; I was put on a Surgical-ward. I knew nothing about surgical cases. One of the Sisters, very upper-class and Miniverish, told me I was 'futile', which was probably quite true. Our patients were mostly head injuries; they were nearly all unconscious, and wet their beds every half-hour or so. They muttered to themselves perpetually; but scarcely ever violently and obscenely as one might have expected. Mostly they murmured 'Oh dear, oh dear' quite quietly, over and over again.

One of the patients was an enormous Basuto. He sat up in bed, supported in Fowler's position, helpless and silent, looking very sad, staring in front of him. Occasionally he smiled, but I never heard him utter a word. One afternoon an orderly came to take his temperature; he was sitting up, as always, silent and expressionless.

'Not got much to say for yourself, George, have you?' the orderly said, feeling for the patient's pulse. The black hand fell back heavily from his own as he lifted it. 'George' had been dead for some time.

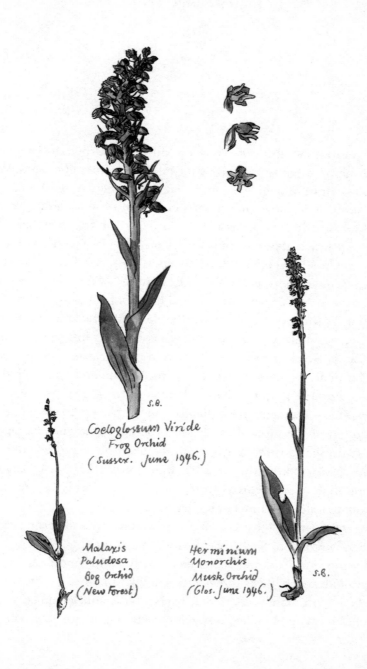

S.B.

Coeloglossum Viride
Frog Orchid
(Sussex. June 1946.)

Malaxis
Paludosa
Bog Orchid
(New Forest)

Herminium
Monorchis
Musk Orchid
(Glos. June 1946.)

S.B.

II

EVERY DAY WE EXPECTED to get a Movement Order: the Unit was waiting to go to Sicily. But the ADMS, so the office said, had made a balls-up; there were no VD units in Sicily, yet we could get no authority to move. In the torrid camp in off-duty hours, or on the wards, I dreamt perpetually of Sicily, trying to remember all I had ever heard about it. Empedocles on Etna, Prosperine at Enna, Aleister Crowley at Cefàlu, *L' Après-midi d'un faune*, D.H. Lawrence and his peasants, the ruins at Agrigentum, Magna Graecia and Pythagoras, Mrs Hurstpierpoint and her 'wild delicious scheme' of visiting Taormina – Sicily became for me a fantastic Land of Heart's Desire, a complex of arbitrary and incongruous images, in which the campaign then raging – the stream of casualties pouring into the hospital, the tales of malaria, scirocco, flies and bugs, syphilis, drought and starvation – had little or no part. *N'importe où, hors du monde* – I would have willingly gone anywhere to escape from Tripoli, from the surgical wards, the broiling August sun beating on our tents, the daily and unvaried ration from Meat and Veg tins.

'So then, I start now to learn Italian, isn't it?' Kurt Schlegel announced. We procured, from the hospital library, a not very adequate Italian grammar, and began to study it.

'*Avete del vino?*' Kurt would say, adding with determination: 'When we come to Sicily, I get drunk, that is sure.'

But it was not till mid-September that our Movement Order did eventually arrive. I was down with sandfly fever and nearly missed the boat. Fortunately we crossed in a Hospital Ship; leaning over the side, as the ship ploughed through the sun-dazzle of a late summer evening, 'Betwixt the Syrtes and soft Sicily', we watched for the first sight of the Promised Land. At length it emerged – a blue, hilly, irregular coastline; at the eastern extremity rose a mountain – conical, formal as a Fujiyama painted on a fan, a child's naive idea of a mountain: it was Mount Etna.

Nearer at hand, on the rising ground above the bay which we were entering, stood what appeared to be a Greek temple, severe and classical in the waning light as the Parthenon itself. Darkness had almost fallen when we docked. The quayside seemed deserted. As we stepped on to the landing stage, a small grey cat scuttled across to greet us. I realised suddenly that this was an Italian – or at least a Sicilian – cat: we were back, at last, in Europe.

We were to spend the night with a detachment of Marines. The trucks dropped us, after a rough ride, before an enormous, minatory facade which we recognised as that of the building which we had taken for some ruined temple. It was not, however, a temple, but an airship hangar. Inside it, in the darkness, the roof seemed as high as the sky itself; eating our Meat and Veg, unrolling our blankets, visiting the improvised latrine, we might as well have been back in Tripoli, or in Palestine, or for that matter at Aldershot. My vision of Sicily had fizzled out – as such visions always do in the army – into this squalid nocturnal process of 'settling-in' to a new billet.

In the morning, however, Sicily was revealed again: the bay of Augusta lay placid and sun-bathed below the hangar; on the horizon Etna had reappeared, an abstract vision of 'mountainousness', formal and serene. A soft, delicious warmth pervaded the morning; nobody seemed to have the least idea what we were to do, or where we were supposed to go. It was as though the soft Sicilian airs had infected us already – infected, indeed, the very mechanics of army procedure, slowing down the tempo of movement, infusing the military machine itself with a kind of *dolce far niente*. The office said the ADMS had dropped another bollock: there ought to have been transport laid on to take us to Catania.

Meanwhile, we moved out of the hangar and prepared to camp in a nearby field. It was almost certain we shouldn't get transport now till the next day – perhaps not for several days. We dropped our blanket-rolls under the olive trees, hanging our mozzy nets from their branches. Olive orchards and fields stretched away towards the rising hills; here and there, farmhouses lay calmly, solidly, like natural features, an indispensable part of the picture's composition. The whole landscape seemed immensely pictorial; yet its 'picturesqueness' was no mere superficies of prettiness, an effect of light or ephemeral vegetation or the viewpoint of the observer, as a 'picturesque' scene would have been in England; here the pictorial effect was achieved by the bare architecture of the landscape which now, at the end of the summer, dried-up and flowerless, was perhaps less conventionally 'pretty' than at any other time of the year.

Compared with English landscapes, this first vision of Sicily was like a Cézanne compared with a fuzzy Victorian watercolour. I had seen the landscape of the Midi; but here, even more than in the landscapes which Cézanne himself had painted, I became aware of the architecture, the 'bare bones' of a natural scene. There was nothing 'soft', after all, I thought, about Sicily: it was a hard land – hard, but with an honesty, a primitive candour which concealed nothing.

Presently the landscape began to be peopled with figures. The first to appear was a small boy. Kurt and I decided to practise our Italian.

'*Avete del vino*?' we asked.

'*Mafeesh vino*,' he replied.

'So then, these bastards learn Arabic already,' exclaimed Kurt, with disgust.

Later on, a little pony-cart drove up laden with barrels. The cart was painted gaily with bright garlands and pictures of saints. The elderly peasant who drove it stopped and greeted us. Yes, we could buy some wine. Sixteen lire a litre. Or perhaps we would like to buy a barrel? No, at the moment we didn't need a barrel. We filled our water bottles; I tasted the wine.

'It's the real thing,' I said to Kurt, as the cool, lovely stuff struck the back of my palate. It was full-bodied yet dry, like a burgundy, but with the salty tang that I remembered from Italian wines in England.

Soon the rest of the Unit had followed our example. We sat in the sun, drinking; and later, walking across the hills, found a farmhouse with a table set out in front of it, under the trees. The padrone invited us to have a drink. We sat under the olives, drinking slowly, and practising painfully our phrases of Italian. In my brain, like an incantation, the words repeated themselves over and over again: 'I am back in Europe; I am in Sicily.'

By midday, when the rations were issued, the entire Unit was drunk. Not for a long time had bully-beef tasted so good as this did, washed down with the first Sicilian wine. Dinner, on this first morning back in Europe, was a kind of celebration. After it, we began to feel sleepy. Some of us unrolled our blankets. Suddenly three trucks appeared from nowhere, and pulled up on the edge of the field: they were our transport.

Somehow we got our kit aboard, and piled in after it; the driver must have been drunk too, for the drive was a nightmare. We were scheduled to pick up a train at a station on the way to Catania: the drivers attempted several short cuts, one of them over a partially demolished bridge. The few members of the Unit who were comparatively sober said that it was the worst moment of their lives. Most of us, fortunately, were too drunk to notice.

We arrived, eventually, at Catania. Needless to say, nobody expected us. The ADMS, they said in the office, had made another balls-up. We should have gone to Syracuse, not to Catania at all.

Next day we went to Syracuse: we were to be attached, it seemed, to No. — General Hospital. This, we found, occupied a half-built lunatic asylum outside the town. There were over two hundred patients waiting for our arrival; they had been waiting for some weeks, it seemed. More were arriving all the time. At present they were being treated by a part-time Medical Officer and a couple of orderlies. There was no sanitation, very little water, and no accommodation. The office said the ADMS had bollocksed things up as usual. It certainly looked like it.

Two days later we had opened up our hospital and started work.

'You'll go on nights,' the staff sergeant told me.

I went on nights by myself: there was nobody else to spare. Soon we had over 400 patients. During the night there were temperatures to take, sulphonamide tablets to distribute, dressings to apply. It was also at night that most of the convoys arrived. These chiefly came from the mainland; sometimes they had been travelling for a week, and many of the patients had developed acute prostatitis or epididymitis as a result of delayed treatment. Often, when they arrived, there was nowhere to put them; on these occasions they lay down in the fields until tents could be erected and stretchers procured.

In the mornings, the sun rose behind Etna, waking the calm, classical landscape to another broiling day. I sat in the office tent, admitting the last of the night's convoy, eating grapes and drinking wine and water out of a rusty tin mug. After breakfast I walked down the dusty road towards Syracuse. Halfway down were the remains of a Greek theatre, and nearby, in a deep lane shadowed by lemons and oleanders, a wine shop. The wine shop was cool and cavernous, with barrels ranged round the walls; the padrona, who served behind the bar, was a massive, severe-looking matron like the Mother of the Gracchi. I sat in the wine shop, looking out on the small garden full of ripening lemons; drinking my wine, and eating grapes. Later, I walked down to the Greek theatre, and sat on the ruined tiers, watching the lizards darting in and out among the vervain and the grape hyacinths.

Then the rainy season began. The hospital tents flooded; sometimes they blew down. The patients increased; our Unit decreased, a section of it having left for the mainland. The advance section, however, could find nowhere to open up: the nightly convoys continued to arrive, in increasing numbers, at Syracuse. The ADMS, they said in the office, had dropped another goolie.

After a month, I went on 'days'.

'I want this man to have hot sitz baths four-hourly,' said the MO one morning.

'I'm sorry, Sir, there's no water. We've hardly enough for the ordinary treatments, and we have to boil that up on the Primus. We've no facilities for heating big quantities, even if we had enough water. The patients on tablets can't get enough, as it is. The office says the ADMS— '

'Yes, I see,' said the MO. He appeared to have been listening carefully to what I was saying. 'Well, the point is, I want this patient to have hot sitz baths four-hourly, so you *will* see he gets them, won't you?'

The work was hard, our conditions appalling; the MOs demanded impossibilities; half the Unit, moreover, was absent; yet the infection of the Sicilian *dolce far niente* persisted: a sense of balminess and easy gaiety pervaded our billets and even the hospital itself. We laughed immoderately at absurdities; and the discomforts of the place were outweighed by an imponderable and irrational happiness.

One day a singular patient was admitted: an elderly Chinaman in the Merchant Navy. He arrived with an enormous trolley, pushed by two Italians, laden with vast quantities of kit, including a bed. It is doubtful if he realised in the least why he was there; he knew not a word of English, but shuffled about the hospital, urinating in unsuitable places, apparently perfectly contented, and wearing upon his face a broad and placid smile.

Charlie Dacres, a Cockney, and a friend of mine and Kurt's, found him irresistibly amusing. This, apparently, the Chinaman (who became known, inevitably, as Who Flung Dung) took as a compliment, which he politely returned by offering to present Charlie with his bed. Charlie as politely refused it; they exchanged cigarettes and grinned and nodded blandly at each other with the greatest friendliness.

One day I went into the treatment tent where Kurt was working. Surrounded by a crowd of other patients, he was trying to explain to Who Flung Dung that he must come for sulphonamide tablets every four hours, at eight o'clock, twelve o'clock, four o'clock, and so on. Black in the face with the effort, poor Kurt pointed to his watch, repeating over and over again to him the hours at which he must attend: the Chinaman stood there, entirely unconcerned, wearing as ever his bland, impenetrable smile, not understanding a word, but replying politely to each new attempt of Kurt's with the only syllable of English which he knew: 'Yiss . . . yiss . . .' The more Kurt stormed, the more polite the Chinaman's smile became.

'So then . . .' Kurt threw at him, finally, his own command of English becoming impaired in the face of such blank incomprehension, 'You come when I say, or you go and get stuffed, you bastard.'

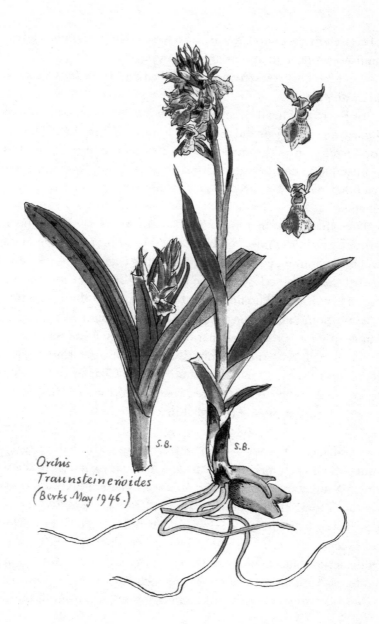

Orchis
Traunsteinerioides
(Berks. May 1946.)

S.B.   S.B.

I related the story to Charlie, who worked in the Irrigation Room. A mischievous light sprang into his eyes.

'Can't have Kurt ill-treating my old china,' he said. 'Oh, no. You just wait.'

For the rest of the day he kept watch, and at intervals of not more than a quarter of an hour, seized hold of Who Flung Dung and conducted him to the entrance of Kurt's tent, motioning him, with unmistakable emphasis, to enter. That evening, Kurt appeared in the billet which the three of us shared, looking more than usually exhausted.

'For what does that bastard Chinaman every ten minutes for —ing treatment come?' he burst out. 'I tell him to come at eight, twelve, four and eight, and now he comes every ten —ing minutes. If they admit bloody Chinamen, why do they not an interpreter ask? He comes and he nods and he smiles, and I think I go mad.'

'Have some *vino*,' suggested Charlie diplomatically, his face as innocently inexpressive as that of the Chinaman himself.

'So then, I get drunk,' Kurt declared, with determination, and thereupon emptied the bottle at a draught. Charlie and I went out to get some more; our laughter, freed from the restraint of Kurt's presence, was explosive and prolonged.

We had made friends with a peasant family, and used to spend most of our evenings with them. The house lay back from the road, down a dusty lane bordered with prickly pears: the children would see us coming down the lane and call *Buona sera*. We sat in the doorway of the house, in the dusk, eating almonds and drinking an excellent red wine from Floridia. Inside the door, the mother sat with her youngest child on her knee; the father sat nearby, at the table, on which the wine bottle gleamed darkly in the light from a primitive lamp, consisting of a wick floating in olive oil; the other children crouched in the doorway, in the dusk. They were the most beautiful people I had ever seen, and the most civilised.

For them, the process of living – on however low a scale, and of however limited a scope – remained an art. I knew, of course, that any of my comrades in the Unit – except perhaps Kurt – would have laughed at me for calling them 'civilised'; for the modern, popular sense of the word has little or no connection with its ancient meaning. Our peasant friends had no lavatories, no wireless, probably their house was bug-ridden; their children would probably grow up illiterate; but their most trivial doings and sayings – a hand waved in greeting, the position in which the mother held her child, the manner, apologetic yet proud and dignified, in which they lamented their poor hospitality – these things revealed them, no less surely than his physical features reveal the Jew, as belonging to a race which deserved, more than most, to be called civilised rather than barbarian.

In mid-October the rains abated somewhat, and a kind of St Martin's Summer occurred. We walked over to bathe at Santa Panagia, a few miles along the coast from Syracuse, on the way to Augusta.

Santa Panagia is possibly not the most beautiful place in the world; but it would be hard, I felt, to find its rival. A small fishing village, built upon two spurs of rock, forming a small cove; rocky slopes rising to the higher ground behind it; and, to seaward, across the calm, enormous bay, the hilly lands beyond Augusta, and behind them, again, towering dimly into the hazy blue, yet preserving its august and formal outline, the immense cone of Mount Etna.

As one approached the village, the first thing one saw, immediately below, outlined against the bright-blue waters of the cove, midway between the two rocky spurs, was the brand-new railway station: a square, bright-pink, 'modernistic' affair, very fascist, and doubtless

a source of much pride to the inhabitants. That station ought
to have spoilt Santa Panagia; but somehow it didn't. Planted in
the midst of a village in Sussex or Somerset, it would have been
frightful; but here, against this solid, classically proportioned
background, it seemed a mere joke, childish but inoffensive, like
the balloon or bicycle which a modern painter such as Chirico or
Rousseau le Douanier will introduce incongruously into an archaic
or 'primitive' landscape.

We bathed in the cove, and afterwards sat on the rocks, drinking
our wine and eating our bread and cheese. The rainy season had
brought a kind of autumnal spring: the paths above the village
were fringed with emerald-green grass, and the stony slopes were
carpeted with 'spring' flowers: tiny white narcissi, a species of
squill, a miniature pink crocus an inch high, yellow ranunculi,
grape hyacinths. Walking back to the hospital, through the
orchards which bounded the road, one expected to see the peaches
and apricots in blossom; but all one saw – for it was autumn, after
all – was the peasants gathering the olives and lemons.

When we returned to the hospital, where reinforcements had
arrived: the office expected a Movement Order to rejoin the forward
section of the Unit. We made up our minds to revisit Santa Panagia
before we left. But the Movement Order arrived a day or two later,
just as the office said it would. We never saw the little cove, with its
crowded cottages and pink railway station, again.

Our Movement Order took us to Taranto, by landing craft. From
there we moved to Bari, thence to Foggia. At Foggia the winter
met us, and it was bitterly cold. The building requisitioned for our
hospital had very few windows left intact; our billets had none.
The billets had formerly been inhabited by the lay-sisters from
a civilian hospital. On the walls hung oleographs of the Sacred
Heart and St Anthony; in the cupboards, however, objects of a

very un-nun-like character were discovered.

'So then, here you are,' exclaimed Kurt, in a triumphant outburst of anti-clericalism, 'even the nuns do not despise the love. I think,' he added reflectively, 'I think they are very sensible, isn't it?'

We were not long at Foggia: but long enough to get the hospital opened up, and working as smoothly as circumstances permitted. Then another Movement Order arrived.

'Can't understand it,' said the corporal clerk. 'The bloody place isn't on the map.'

'What's it called?' I asked.

He spelt out the letters, painfully. The name was quite unfamiliar. 'Must be a code,' said the corporal. 'Looks to me as if somebody's made another balls-up.'

'Probably,' I suggested, 'it's the ADMS.'

But for once ADMS had done nothing of the kind. The transport duly arrived, and we set off. The journey had a curious paranoid quality, like a story by Kafka. Nobody knew quite where we were going, or why. Hour after hour the trucks lumbered on, further and further into the country. The land fell away around us as we began to climb; soon we were up in the hills, coasting along narrow roads between rocky banks sprinkled thinly with snow. Late in the afternoon we arrived: a solitary building presented itself, among fields, on a hill. Across a valley, a village perched on another hill. All round the building was a sea of mud and half-melted snow. An inscription over the doorway announced that the place had been a *Scuola Agricola*, an Agricultural College.

'Cor, what a dump,' said Charlie Dacres.

'So then, chum, you've had it,' Kurt remarked, with a certain vindictive satisfaction.

'I wish I could have five minutes with that ADMS,' said the corporal clerk.

III

BUT BY THE TIME we had opened up the hospital once more and were settled into our billets, the place didn't seem so bad. It was at the southern extremity of the Abruzzi, in the Vastese region. On the first clear day after our arrival an enormous snow-covered mountain revealed itself to northward: it was the Majella. From beyond its towering whiteness we could hear, when the wind was favourable, the distant thunder of the guns bombarding Pescara.

The weather turned sunny and warm, and lasted for three weeks; then the winter returned. But on the intermittent fine days, the slow, furtive approach of spring revealed itself. I took to going for long walks: on my first outing, it was pleasing to find *Helleborus foetidus* growing in the hedges. Kurt and I and Charlie began to make friends with the peasants; they were cautious but friendly. We sat outside their houses drinking wine in the afternoon sun. It seemed hard to believe there was a war on.

'I think,' said Kurt, 'this will be a good place.'

Ringed with its low, soft-contoured hills, topped with remote villages, the country had an oddly static, formal air: it suggested, in this lenten weather, with the snow still streaking the hilltops and lingering under hedges, some emblematic vision of winter in an illuminated missal or Book of Hours. Superficially, the landscape resembled northern Europe rather than central Italy: the level tillage, the copses of young oaks, the cart-tracks fringed with thorn and bramble – even the coltsfoot flowering in the waste patches – gave it an almost English air. Only when the eye encountered the changeless, classic olives, or the hilltop village with the snow-covered Majella beyond, did the view suggest Italy.

Yet even in these weeks of almost unrelieved greyness and intermittent rain, the landscape never quite lost that lucid, sharp-edged quality peculiar to the South. Its 'northern' air was elusive, fleeting. These fields and woods declared themselves with too much frankness; they had none of that mysteriousness, that hint of the *au delà*, which lurks always in the English countryside, even in the Home Counties, and especially during the winter and early spring. Here, the grey skies, the snow, the dripping copses, existed, so to speak, in their own right: details, merely, of the winter landscape. Turn the page, and the scene would change to Spring, another and equally formal vision (the Gothic comparison recurs) of the monkish chronicler.

As with the landscape, so with the figures: they recurred in each static, gilt-bordered version of the identical scene – actors in this country chronicle, employed in tasks suited to the season. Now, in March, in the copse of young oak trees which clothed the slope by the village, the peasants – seen as blue and red blobs in the middle-distance, bright against the dun, neutral background – were occupied in chopping wood for fuel. Nearby, at the farmhouse door, a woman sat with bent, kerchiefed head, babe at breast, half-watching the scene before her; and our eyes, lighting upon her calm, immobile figure, demanded something which seemed unaccountably missing; the gilded, expensive nimbus about her bent head, the painter's pious collage upon this rural and naturalistic landscape.

It had snowed for a week: and suddenly the wind came soft and the brown and green patchwork of fields, the silver-grey olives were revealed again. The sun at midday was warm as an English May, the stream-side was miraculously fringed with white polyanthus narcissi, their heavy scent evoking the atmosphere of English drawing rooms. In the copse, white crocuses sprang like sudden stars, and among the undergrowth crimson anemones flickered like strontium flames. Next day the snow returned, powdering with soft precision the fields and woods, formal and pictorial as the snow in a Victorian glass paperweight. The anemones, the narcissi were a freak, a vision of Spring in Winter; fleeting as the sudden, never-to-be-repeated lyric thrown off by some dull, timeserving pedant; a promise not to be fulfilled in this winterland, this never-turned page of the missal, lying open on the lectern, showing only Winter: the reader away at the Wars, perhaps dead by now.

Yet the slow invasion of spring continued, becoming gradually more insistent: infecting the landscape like the advance of some recurrent fever. Violets succeeded the anemones in the copses, the thin, stripling oaks burst into sudden leaf overnight; and then, walking into the nearest copse after an interval of some days, I saw the first cyclamens; tongues of rosy flame straining upwards from the still-leafless ground, as though in celebration of some Plutonic pentecost. Soon the wood floor was covered with them: mingled, here and there, with the blue mountain anemone, which used to grow in the gardens of our Kentish village. In the cornfields, the gladiolus grew as it had grown in Cyrenaica; and on waste patches or in the young corn, the grape hyacinth spread its drifts of ultramarine among the drooping yellow bells of the wild tulip.

Here, as in Africa, the flowers were near enough to those of northern Europe to strike a familiar note. In the woods, I had been watching some orchid leaves. According to an Italian Flora, which I had unearthed in the *Scuola Agricola*, the military orchid ought to occur in these parts. The broad, unspotted leaves, abundant in the woods nearby, were promising; but the next few weeks revealed their secret: they were not, after all, the military, but *Orchis purpurea*, the

Neotinea Intacta
(Co. Galway.)
12. 5. 1940.

Aceras Anthropop.
Man Orchid
(Kent 26.5. 1940, 31.5. 1939)

orchid which, on a June evening nearly thirty years before, nameless, then, and unrecognised, had been brought to me by Mr Bundock.

Another orchid, however, grew nearby: so much smaller that I took it to be an *Ophrys*, the bee orchid, perhaps, or the spider orchid. It was later in flowering: I decided to keep my eye on it.

We were not hard-worked at all: patients came in manageable quantities, and the two sections of the Unit were reunited. Major Wilmott was more *alakefak* than ever; we arranged our duty-times as it suited us.

Kurt, Charlie and I spent much time with the peasants. We had treated some of them at the hospital, and they showed their gratitude by frequent offers of wine and eggs.

One house had aroused our curiosity for some time: it lay some little distance away across the fields, and for some reason we had never visited it. One day, however, just before Easter, we decided to investigate it.

'I think we find some good *vino*,' said Kurt.

We set off – Kurt, Charlie and I. Half an hour's walk brought us to the house. It lay by itself at the side of a cart-track: similar to the other houses in the neighbourhood, but larger than most. A flight of steps led up the southern wall to an upper room; there was a small vineyard nearby, and a tall, conical haystack, which had been sliced into at need like a cake, and began to look top-heavy. With its white walls and rust-red pantiled roof, the house looked friendly and welcoming in the spring sunshine.

A small boy, playing in the yard, looked at us curiously. Presently he sidled up to us.

'*Sigarette? Cioccolata?*' he asked hopefully.

'We go to ask some *vino*,' said Kurt. '*Avete del vino?*' he asked.

'Si, si,' the boy answered with a charming smile.

We followed him round to the doorway on the other side. A woman appeared at the door: tall, broad-bosomed, brown-faced, dressed in nondescript clothes which had once been gaily coloured, and still hung gracefully upon her straight, stalwart body. On her head was a bright-coloured kerchief.

'*Buon giorno*,' she said, with a curious, dramatic sweep of her arm: a stylised, almost operatic gesture of welcome, at once proud and humble, which seemed to imply that we were free to take possession, if we wished, of the entire farm, such as it was. She accompanied the movement with a broad, delightful smile, revealing two rows of strong, white teeth.

'*Dov'è il padrone, Signora, per cortesia?*' asked Kurt.

The padrone was working in the fields, she replied. '*Cosa vuole?*'

'*Se avete un mezzo-litre di vino . . ?*'

'*Si, si. S'accommodino*,' she exclaimed, and immediately pushed forward three little wooden chairs for us.

'In moment her husband works in the fields,' Kurt explained to Charlie, whose Italian was almost nonexistent. 'But she gives us wine.'

We sat down, and presently the woman returned with a jug of wine and three glasses. I poured out the wine, and we all said '*Saluti*.' The woman watched us as we drank; so did the little boy, still on the look-out for chocolate.

'*E buono?*' she asked.

'*Molto buono*,' we said.

It was true: the wine was a *vino nero* – dark, sour, potent, with a purplish glint when held to the light; much better than most of the local wines, which were light and watery, like alcoholic lemonade.

We sat in the sunshine, drinking it slowly, and talking a little to the woman. Kurt did most of the talking: he spoke ungrammatically, but with the confidence of a Central European. I was more shy, being English, and had to think up my phrases carefully. Charlie contented himself with saying '*molto buono*' and playing with the child.

Presently other children appeared, stealing up like shy birds whom the sight of us had driven away: another little boy, a girl of fifteen strikingly like her mother, and another, younger girl, perhaps eleven or twelve, blonde and uncannily beautiful.

We were introduced: the elder girl was called Assunta, the younger Graziella, the two boys Leonardo and Giovanni.

'*Quanti bambini?*' Kurt asked.

'*Cinque*,' the woman replied, holding up the five fingers of one hand; adding that one, the eldest son, was working with his father.

'She is beautiful,' Kurt remarked, of Graziella.

'Like a Botticelli,' I said.

'*Volete ancora?*' the woman asked.

'I think we drink some more,' Kurt said, with decision.

'Too bloody true we will,' said Charlie. 'Best *vino* I've had since we came to this place.'

Kurt asked the woman for more, explaining that we would pay for it. '*Non fa niente*,' she assured us.

'We give her cigarettes,' Kurt suggested.

We pulled out our cases, and contributed ten each. Kurt handed them to the woman.

'*Per il padrone*,' he said.

'*Eh. . . . Lei è molto gentile*,' she said, with a half-protesting gesture, and hurried to bring more wine. This time she brought, in addition, three pieces of bread, some cheese and some sprouts of fennel.

Did we like *finocchi*? she asked.

We said we liked it.

It was not good to drink without eating, she added apologetically.

We sat over the second jug of wine, relaxed and happy in the warm sun. In front of the house, fields sloped down to a little wooded valley; beyond this, the country stretched away flatly to the low hills, capped by small villages. The brightly coloured landscape had a curious quality of naïveté and innocence. Two cypresses, a few yards from the house, divided the picture abruptly into sections, like the divisions of a triptych. In the middle-distance, figures moved across the fields, hoeing, as though in a picture by Millet. Perhaps the padrone was among them.

Presently, the beautiful child, Graziella, who had wandered off, reappeared, carrying a little bunch of flowers: grape hyacinths, narcissi and yellow tulips. These she presented to us, gravely smiling, then shyly backed away again.

'I've a feeling we're getting well in here,' Charlie said. 'What say we ask for some *parster shooter*?'

'She'd do it,' I said. 'Go on, Kurt. You ask her. Not today, though. I'm on at five o'clock, you know.'

'No, I don't ask. Always you want me to talk bloody Italian. You ask her yourself.'

Finally Kurt and I together approached the topic with as much delicacy as our Italian allowed.

'*E possibile mangiare qui, alla vostra casa*?' we began, and, antiphonally, pressed our point: *pasta asciutta*, perhaps a salad, some eggs. We were so tired of army food, we explained: we wanted to eat well, *mangiare bene all'Italiana*.

The woman shrugged her shoulders. They had so little food, now, in Italy; the *tedeschi* had taken everything – cattle, poultry, wine, anything they could carry – *e niente pagato*. It was different in peacetime; but now, *in tempo di guerra*. . . .

'Heavy going,' I said to Kurt. 'We'll have to use bribery. Jimmy'll give us a tin of bully out of the store, if we get him some *vino*.'

Kurt nodded, a glint coming into his eye.

'We make business,' he said.

At mention of *carne*, the signora obviously began to weaken. She would ask the padrone. I added that I would bring some clothes: I had some old civvy vests and pants in my kit which I never wore. The outlook began to seem more hopeful.

At that moment, the padrone himself appeared, with his eldest son. The father was short, with a pleasant, sharp-featured face and beady-black eyes; he wore a battered trilby, and a brightly coloured handkerchief round his neck. The son, about sixteen, was beautiful. If Graziella was Renaissance, Umberto was something archaic: a faun from a Greek vase-painting.

The father was presented with the cigarettes. He immediately called for more wine, and we all sat down again, inside this time. Charlie came in, and the atmosphere became distinctly festive. I wished I wasn't on duty at five: I began to feel rather drunk, and refused any more wine. The bare, whitewashed room was very clean; bunches of drying tomatoes hung from ceiling-beams, and a few salami. In the open stone hearth a fire of olive-wood was blazing, and a vast cauldron hung over it, waiting for the pasta, which lay ready for cooking, in a floury pile, on the scrubbed wooden table.

The padrone was very friendly. He wanted to know all about the war: we were soldiers, we should know. We explained that we were medical orderlies, *croce rossa*, *non combattere*. He looked half-convinced. *Ieri sera molto boom-boom-boom*, he insisted: over there, beyond the mountains – pointing northwards. There was a big battle, we said: beyond Pescara, on the way to Bologna. We were lucky, he said, not to fight. Had we many *feriti* in our hospital? No, we only dealt with medical cases, we said, *ammalati*. Our hospital was in the *Scuola Agricola* across the fields. We tried to explain, in our faulty Italian, that we were a VD Unit.

Time was getting short, and after a discreet interval we broached the subject of food again. Yes, certainly we must come, he said: next Sunday was Easter – *una grande festa*. It was also a special feast for the family – Leonardo, the second son, was to make his first communion. The cigarettes had done their work. We scraped up a few more for Umberto, and prepared to leave. This we were not allowed to do until we had drunk another glass of wine. We repeated, for the padrone's benefit, our promises to the signora: we would bring a tin of bully, some old clothes, some chocolate for the *bambini*. Suddenly made bold by our success with her husband, the signora took me aside and half-whispered that if we could see our way to bring a *coperta* as well. . . .

'They want a blanket,' I said to Kurt.

'They've had it,' Kurt said. 'I don't go over the wall for two years, that's sure.'

'We've all those buckshee ones from Foggia,' I pointed out. 'They've no check on them.'

'I'm not mad,' said Kurt.

'Plenty of blankets,' said Charlie, who had been putting back *vino* on the quiet. 'I'll bring her one.' He turned to the signora. '*Si, si,*' he assured her, '*molto* blankets – what the —ing hell are blankets?'

'She understands all right.'

'Certainly she does,' said Kurt. 'Don't you be worried.'

'*Io portare molto* – you know, blankets,' Charlie insisted. 'Compree?'

'*Si, si. Troppo gentile,*' the signora exclaimed, rewarding Charlie with one of her broad, maternal smiles. She was like a Demeter, an Earth Goddess, I thought.

'See, she's taken a fancy to me,' Charlie said proudly. 'I told you we'd get well in.'

We promised to come at two o'clock on Easter Sunday, and with difficulty left the house. At the last minute, Assunta presented us each with a little bunch of violets, and Umberto, no doubt on instructions from the padrone, brought up a bottle of wine, which I stuffed into the front of my battledress. The family watched us out of sight. Looking back across the fields, we saw them standing in the doorway, waving. The house, with its two dark cypresses, stood out brilliantly against the sun-flooded landscape: it seemed like a symbol of happiness, a vision of the good life.

The problem was to get the blanket out of the billets without being seen. 'It is better if you take it at night,' Kurt advised.

'Is it —' retorted Charlie. 'Looks too bloody suspicious. Much better to take it in daylight.'

'So then, Private Dacres, you go over the wall,' Kurt predicted with morbid relish. 'That is sure.'

'And you —ing come with me, Private —ing Schlegel, RAMC,' said Charlie with gusto. 'It's all right, mate, I wasn't born yesterday.'

We walked out of the billets just before two o'clock on Easter Sunday. Charlie had rolled up the blanket – one of a buckshee issue, unchecked, which we had acquired at Foggia – in a bundle, adequately disguised, to unsuspicious eyes, by several layers of dirty linen. Kurt also carried a bundle: he had compromised with his scruples sufficiently to part with a couple of khaki drill shirts which weren't shown on his 1157 form. My own bundle, innocent enough to all appearances, contained the cast-off civvy underclothes which I'd bought in Cairo; in the front of my battledress was a tin of bully for which I had bargained with Jimmy James, the Ration Corporal.

We stepped jauntily out of the hospital entrance, looking rather consciously innocent, and walked straight into the staff sergeant.

S.B.

M.B.

Orchis Simia
Monkey Orchid
(Oxfordshire. June 1946.)

'Where're you blokes off to?' he said.

My heart sank like a stone. Just our luck, I thought. If the staff sergeant was in a bad mood, he might quite easily make things awkward. He flogged too much himself, as we all knew, to regard our bundles without suspicion.

'What's in all them —ing bundles?' he asked.

I mentally decided to unroll my own first, if he pressed the point: there was nothing in mine he could pick on. I hoped he wouldn't ask to see Charlie's.

'We take our laundry to a farm,' Kurt explained.

'That's right,' Charlie agreed. 'The old *biancheria*, you know.'

The staff sergeant grunted.

'Remember,' he said, 'if I find anyone in this Unit flogging stuff, I'm coming down heavy on them. Very heavy.'

'Ain't got — all to flog,' Charlie said, nervousness making him cheeky.

The staff sergeant gave him a nasty look.

'Is anyone on duty here?' he asked. 'Who's in the clinic, eh?'

'Smudge is relieving me,' Charlie said. 'It's my half-day.'

'Who's in the lab?'

'Nobby does the lab in moment,' Kurt replied. 'He has two dark-grounds and one instillation, then finish.'

'What about the office?'

'Mac's there,' I said. 'He's on long-trot today.'

'Well, don't get too pissed. If I had my way I'd have those bloody *casas* all put out of bounds. You'd think this was a bloody rest-camp, instead of a pox-joint.'

We escaped.

'Miserable sod,' Charlie muttered. 'Just 'cos he doesn't like *vino*.'

'He likes *finocchi*,' I said. 'We might bring him some.'

'— him.'

The day was brilliant and cloudless, hot but with a fresh breeze. We walked through a field breast-deep already with pink clover. In the little copse at the field's edge, nightingales were singing. In the meadow beyond the clover field the stream-side was still fringed with white narcissi.

'It's a wonderful country,' Charlie said. 'Bloody wonderful. Garden flowers growing wild, and all.' Kurt and I laughed.

'Three months ago you were saying how bloody awful it was,' I reminded him.

'I didn't know it then.'

'So now you stay in Italy *dopo la guerra* and marry a nice signorina, isn't it? 'Kurt suggested.

'I might if I hadn't a wife and kids in Blighty,' Charlie agreed.

Our way led through the copse, on the slope of a little valley, where I had been watching a colony of orchids. Today, after only a week's absence, I was amazed to find them in blossom: their pinkish tufted spikes were scattered over the copse, among the dwarf yellow genista and purple gromwell. I examined them; they were not, as I imagined, a species of *Ophrys*, but a particularly luxuriant form of *Orchis simia*, the monkey orchid: the very plant which, more than twenty years before, had arrived at St Ethelbert's in a brown-paper parcel and had been stuffed, unceremoniously, into a toothglass in the dormitory.

Now, as then, I felt impelled to suppress – or at least to modify – the pleasure which the sight of it gave me: not that Kurt and Charlie would have minded in the least, but one is apt to be self-conscious about such private enthusiasms, which one cannot share. The Italian monkey orchid, as a matter of fact, differed considerably from its English counterpart: it was more robust, with broader divisions of the lip. Still, it was undoubtedly *Orchis simia*, and to find it, on this Easter day, when we were on our way to a *festa*, when the whole countryside, indeed, seemed already to be flooded with a warm delightful sense of happiness – to find it thus had the effect of suddenly crystallizing my own contentment, like the final grain of some mineral which, dropped into the beaker, is enough to saturate the solution.

Growing among the other 'monkeys' I observed one which was not yet in flower; much larger and more robust than the rest; it differed from them, also, in having a long, cylindrical spike. There seemed, I thought, little doubt that this, at last, was the true military orchid. A day or two more would decide the point; and meanwhile, after gathering some specimens of the monkey, I rejoined the others.

We came out on to the track again, by a little row of houses. Some of the families were standing outside, wearing their best finery for Easter. They greeted us with smiles and welcoming gestures.

'*Buona Pasqua*' they said; Christ might have risen, this very morning, for their special benefit: so happy did they seem. It was hard to believe there was a war on. Even as we passed the house, a muffled rumble came from over the mountains – away beyond the Majella, white and austere on the horizon.

A family with whom we were friendly – we had treated the daughter for malaria – refused to let us pass without a glass of wine. Their neighbours followed suit. We were not allowed to go on till we had drunk a glass at each house in the row. When at last we arrived at the farmhouse where we were invited, we were, as Charlie said, 'Well away.'

We had been asked for two o'clock, but time in Italy is elastic, and dinner was far from being ready. The signora was busy with pots and pans; Assunta, the eldest daughter, was cutting up the pasta into long strips like tapeworms. The other children sat with the padrone just inside the door. At the hearth sat an ancient woman whom we had not met before: grey-haired, dressed in drab, ragged clothes, she looked like a benevolent witch. Introduced to us as *la nonna*, she croaked an unintelligible greeting, in dialect, and went on with her task of stoking the fire with olive wood. Leonardo, who had taken his first communion that morning, was the hero of the occasion: with his face scrubbed, and wearing a little suit of snow-white linen, he looked cherubic and very self-important. With immense pride he showed us his *Ricordo della prima comunione* – a three-colour print showing an epicene Christ surrounded by very bourgeois-looking children, all with blond hair.

With many nods, gestures and whispered thanks (as though the entire Corps of Military Police lay in ambush round the house) the blanket, the bully and the underclothes were secreted in a back room. A two-litre flask of wine appeared as though by magic: this was not good wine, the padrone explained; later we would drink good wine, *del vino tanto buono.*

It was good enough for us. We had had no dinner, and must have already drunk nearly a litre apiece on the way. We distributed cigarettes to the padrone and Umberto, and chocolate to the children. Leonardo received six bars all to himself, and Giovanni, who resented his brother's hour of glory, burst into tears. He was consoled with half a glass of wine.

'Wish I'd been brought up like that,' said Charlie.

'It's all for a cock, these bloody Catholic *festas*,' said Kurt, who, being both Jew and Communist, objected to Easter on religious and political grounds.

'Ah, you miserable old bugger,' exclaimed Charlie, and, lifting Giovanni on to his knee, consoled him further with an extra piece of chocolate.

Presently the meal began: the steaming, fragrant tomato juice was poured over the two enormous bowls of pasta and we sat down round the table.

'*Ancora, ancora*' the padrone insisted, before we had finished our first platefuls. '*Oggi festa – mangiamo molto per Pasqua.*'

After the pasta there was chicken cooked with tomato and pepperoni. This was followed by salami fried with eggs. Then came a dish of pork with young peas. Roast sparrows followed, and afterwards a salad. At about the salami stage, after several false alarms, the 'good' wine was produced: two bottles the size of magnums.

It was a Homeric meal.

Kurt, who had been a student in Vienna before the war, quoted Homer very appropriately, but in German, which nobody understood. Charlie was trying to sing *Lili Marlene* in Italian to Graziella, who sat on his knee. Umberto produced an ancient concertina and began to play it. Kurt, forgetting Homer, started to sing a very sad Austrian folksong. The padrone, for my benefit, kept up a running commentary on the proceedings, comparing the occasion unfavourably with Easters before the war.

'*Prima della guerra era bella, bellissima,*' he insisted. Today everyone was poor. '*E sempre la miseria.*' The Germans had taken everything. It could hardly be called a *festa* at all. He was ashamed: ashamed to offer such an Easter meal to his guests, and mortified, moreover, that Leonardo's first communion should be celebrated so wretchedly. '*Siamo poveri, poveri – noi contadini. Eh, la guerra – quando finirà?*'

I was not only extremely drunk by this time, but I had never eaten so much in my life. So far as I was concerned, Leonardo's first-communion party had been more than adequate.

Presently Umberto struck up a tarantella, and the whole family, as though at a given signal, took the floor. We all paired off, indifferent as to sex, and bobbed and jigged in time to the music. Charlie insisted on taking *la nonna* for his partner; I danced with the signora. I found to my surprise that I was perfectly steady on my feet. Moreover, it seemed that I had been dancing the tarantella all my life. Gravely, wearing her calm Demeter-like smile, the signora advanced and retreated, hands on hips, bobbed and circled and bowed, all with a goddess-like dignity. Her brown face, beneath her coloured kerchief, was as calm as though she were at Mass; only a beatific happiness irradiated it, as though Christ indeed were risen. She seemed immensely aware, too, of her own personal fulfilment: she had given pleasure to her man, borne him healthy children and (more recently) cooked a dinner fit for those gods whose Olympian peer she seemed.

The music became faster, the dancing less restrained. The padrone whirled about like a ballet dancer; Giovanni, still taking a rather disgruntled view of the occasion, did a little dance by himself in the corner. Leonardo didn't dance at all: he stood at the doorway and watched the proceedings with the distant air of one who has, that very morning, eaten the body of Christ for the first time. The two girls, Assunta and Graziella, danced a little apart: separated, it seemed, from the rest of us by a mysterious barrier, a mutual understanding; it was as though they were priestesses, gravely celebrating the godhead of their mother. Umberto sat in a corner, with his concertina: an archaic, sculptured faun, younger and older than anybody else in the room.

At last we could bear it no longer, and staggered out into the late afternoon sun, to cool off. Charlie's face was scarlet, his battledress and shirt gaped open, showing a pink, damp expanse of skin. Kurt's hair had fallen over his square, heavy-browed face: he looked like Beethoven would have looked if he had ever got seriously drunk. I told him so.

'Ach, I could write great symphonies in moment,' he declared. 'I am great *Musiker*. Too bloody true I am, you old sod.'

'You're a fat Austrian c—,' Charlie remarked happily.

'It is pity for you I am not, my friend,' Kurt replied. Umberto came out, his concertina still slung over his shoulder.

He took my hand.

'*Sei felice?*' he asked, his teeth flashing white in his brown face.

'*Sono felice*' I said.

Beyond the twin cypresses the country lay flooded in the warm, slanting light. Away on the horizon, hill upon hill lay revealed in the evening radiance, each topped with its fairytale village or castle. In the oak copse nearby, where the monkey orchid grew, a chorus of nightingales shouted. Graziella had run into the field, and was gathering a bunch of white narcissi.

'*Eh, la guerra. Quando finirà?*'

It was the padrone. He looked sadly across the fields. '*Siamo poveri, poveri,*' he added, as if to himself.

There was a war, they were poor, the landlords in Naples or Rome ground them underfoot, their children were uneducated, the priests were paid to keep them in ignorance . . . I knew it all: I had heard Kurt, the Communist, expound it all in Sicily – with conviction, with passion, and at length. Yet I knew also that with these people, on this Easter day, I felt happier, I felt a more genuine sense of the joy of life than ever before.

At last we prepared to leave. Farewells were protracted, and delayed by innumerable afterthoughts in the form of presents and souvenirs: a bottle of wine in case we were thirsty on the way, another for when we got home, one more because it was the 'good' wine, the special wine for Leonardo's first communion. A fourth bottle was added for some further, rather complicated, reason: perhaps it was to drink Leonardo's health tomorrow. A bundle of *finocchi* was produced for the staff sergeant, whose partiality for it we had mentioned. Pieces of Easter cake were pressed upon us for our friends who had not been to the party. A salami was offered by the signora in case we were hungry in the night – we had had a poor meal after all, she said. Bunches of narcissi and violets could not be refused. Umberto even offered a loaf of bread, in case we should have none with which to eat the salami. A pot of some conserve made of pig's blood was proffered by *la nonna*, because a pig had been killed recently.

Our tunics bulging with bottles, our hands clutching *finocchi* and narcissi (and in my own case, a bunch of monkey orchids), we started out across the fields. Halfway, we were overtaken by Umberto with a dozen new-laid eggs. When at last we reached the hospital and staggered across the yard in front of it, we observed the staff sergeant standing before the entrance exactly where we had left him. He was accompanied by MacDowd, the corporal clerk, and Smudger Smith. Their mouths opened, they stared. Then Smudge began to laugh; Mac began to laugh too. Only the staff sergeant kept his countenance: he looked as black as thunder.

''Ere you are, Staff: 'ere's the mustard and —ing cress for you,' Charlie bawled, and advanced towards the staff sergeant, proffered the bundle of *finocchi*. Unfortunately for the success of the gesture, he tripped over a stone and fell flat on his face: the bottle of wine secreted in his tunic smashed noisily, and spilt itself, like some sudden and appalling haemorrhage, over the gravel.

A quiver which might have been a smile flickered over the staff sergeant's prim grey face.

'You'd better get straight into your —ing billets and get to —ing bed before the Old Man sees you,' he said.

In the billets that night I said to Kurt: 'You can say what you like, these people know how to enjoy themselves. They may be politically uneducated and downtrodden and priest-ridden and all the rest of it, but they know how to live.'

'Too bloody true,' said Charlie, who was finishing off the wine.

Kurt sat up in bed, looking more than ever like Beethoven after a night out.

'So then, have you forgotten?' he asked, with the ominous air of a minor prophet. 'You think they give you all that for nothing? You are —ing stupid, both of you.'

''Course I'm stupid. Who wouldn't be after all that?' Charlie commented, and let out a satisfied fart.

'Do you not realise to what you owe this *festa*?' Kurt pursued.

'Well, what?'

'To *una coperta*, one blanket, property of the —ing British Army. To that you owe your bloody *festa*, isn't it?'

'Too bloody true,' Charlie agreed. 'But it was cheap at the price. Wasn't it?' he appealed to me.

'Yes, it was cheap,' I said thinking of the signora dancing like a goddess, the wine and the sunshine and the flowers, and, beyond the dark cypresses, beyond the copse loud with nightingales where I had found the monkey orchid, the sun-flooded country rolling away towards the distant hills.

IV

A FEW DAYS LATER I returned to the copse to look at the plant which I believed to be the military orchid. It proved, after all, to be only a 'gigantic' form of *Orchis simia*: the lip divisions were too narrow, their colouring too pale for even the most wishfully thinking botanist to think otherwise.

I sat in the copse, listening to the nightingales: realising for the first time, too (for how often does one ever see a nightingale in England?) that Swinburne's 'brown bright nightingale' was an exact description. Around me, the pink spikes of the monkey orchid flaunted themselves bravely, with none of the coyness of their English counterparts, among the broom and purple gromwell. Other orchids lurked in the copse, too – the lady, the green man, the late spider; a gathering of notabilities which, assembled here merely by the principles of Italian ecology, I could never have seen together in England, except perhaps in Mr Bickersteth's wild flower show at Bedales.

Across the little valley, by the farmhouse where we had gone on Easter Sunday, I could see, from where I sat, Leonardo and Giovanni playing round the doorway; and presently the signora herself emerged to spread out some snowy bundles of linen upon the bushes in the garden. She stood for a moment, framed between the two pillars of the cypresses, and, catching sight of me across the valley, waved her hand with a fine, sweeping gesture. Presently I would walk across the valley, and enter the cool, whitewashed kitchen; the padrone would be coming in from the fields, and we should drink some wine. I thought that, one day, I should like to come back and live here; or was the sense of happiness which permeated this countryside merely, as Kurt would insist, an illusion? Was one sentimentalising one's impressions, like any tripper? It was possible; but I chose not to think so. I picked the 'gigantic' plant of the monkey, and walked slowly across the valley towards the house.

'So then, we go,' announced Kurt when I arrived back at the hospital. A signal had arrived; we were to close down the hospital, and be prepared to move off at forty-eight hours' notice.

'It's a bloody shame,' said Charlie. 'Just as we're getting well in.'

'Before we go we take another blanket to that *casa*,' Kurt suggested recklessly. 'Then they give us another *festa*, isn't it?'

It was some weeks before we finally departed. But at last, one brilliant, windless morning, the trucks arrived. We piled in; for most of us it was just another move. Leonardo and Giovanni had trotted across the fields to say goodbye. We gave them some chocolate, and some cigarettes for papa. At last the trucks moved off, down the white dusty road: past our farmhouse, past the little copse where I had found the orchids. The house was on a slight rise, and its red roof, flanked by the two cypresses, remained clearly visible for the first five miles of our journey: beckoning to us across the fields and wooded valleys with a promise of happiness which we must ignore, an invitation which we would never again be able to accept. All that remained would be the brown, dried skeletons of the orchids which I had found in the copse: the lady, the late spider and the monkey; and, among the specimens of the latter, that taller, robust plant which, before it was in flower, had so tantalisingly raised my hopes, and which, if I chose to base my identification upon Linnaeus, Bentham and Hooker or Colonel Mackenzie, might be considered to be the military orchid, but was, as a matter of fact, *Orchis simia*.

Almost, but not quite.

Orchis Militaris
Military Orchid   Epipogon Aphyllum

from drawings in Correvon's Album des Orchidées d'Europe.

Please contact Little Toller Books
to join our mailing list or for more information
on current and forthcoming titles.

Nature Classics Library

IN THE COUNTRY *Kenneth Allsop*
THE JOURNAL OF A DISAPPOINTED MAN *W.N.P. Barbellion*
THROUGH THE WOODS *H.E. Bates*
MEN AND THE FIELDS *Adrian Bell*
THE MILITARY ORCHID *Jocelyn Brooke*
ISLAND YEARS, ISLAND FARM *Frank Fraser Darling*
SWEET THAMES RUN SOFTLY *Robert Gibbings*
A SHEPHERD'S LIFE *W.H. Hudson*
WILD LIFE IN A SOUTHERN COUNTY *Richard Jefferies*
FOUR HEDGES *Clare Leighton*
LETTERS FROM SKOKHOLM *R.M. Lockley*
THE UNOFFICIAL COUNTRYSIDE *Richard Mabey*
RING OF BRIGHT WATER *Gavin Maxwell*
THE SOUTH COUNTRY *Edward Thomas*
SALAR THE SALMON *Henry Williamson*

Also Available

THE LOCAL *Edward Ardizzone & Maurice Gorham*
A long-out-of-print celebration of London's pubs
by one of Britain's most-loved illustrators.

LITTLE TOLLER BOOKS
Stanbridge Wimborne Minster Dorset BH21 4JD
Telephone: 01258 840549
ltb@dovecotepress.com
www.dovecotepress.com